Inner Silence/ Inner Rage to Inner Peace

A Memoir

Kathleen Kelley Bonfilio

BALBOA.PRESS
A DIVISION OF HAY HOUSE

Balboa Press books may be ordered through booksellers or by contacting:

Balboa Press
A Division of Hay House
1663 Liberty Drive
Bloomington, IN 47403
www.balboapress.com
844-682-1282

Because of the dynamic nature of the Internet, any web addresses or links contained in this book may have changed since publication and may no longer be valid. The views expressed in this work are solely those of the author and do not necessarily reflect the views of the publisher, and the publisher hereby disclaims any responsibility for them.

The author of this book does not dispense medical advice or prescribe the use of any technique as a form of treatment for physical, emotional, or medical problems without the advice of a physician, either directly or indirectly. The intent of the author is only to offer information of a general nature to help you in your quest for emotional and spiritual well-being. In the event you use any of the information in this book for yourself, which is your constitutional right, the author and the publisher assume no responsibility for your actions.

Any people depicted in stock imagery provided by Getty Images are models, and such images are being used for illustrative purposes only. Certain stock imagery © Getty Images.

Print information available on the last page.

ISBN: 978-1-9822-5703-3 (sc)
ISBN: 978-1-9822-5705-7 (hc)
ISBN: 978-1-9822-5704-0 (e)

Library of Congress Control Number: 2020920746

Balboa Press rev. date: 10/28/2020

This is my story. The events described are based upon my recollections and are true. Out of the respect for their privacy, I have changed the names and places of the people who appear in these pages.

DEDICATIONS

To Hawk Hickman and Barbara Wolf for all the numerous hours spent helping me make this book a reality.

And to my special son Salvatore, who has recently passed on. His encouragement for me to continue this book has been my savior. I'm sure he is looking down at me with a big smile.

CONTENTS

PREFACE

When I first started out to write this book, a thought occurred to me. *Why am I writing this book? What am I trying to accomplish?* I first thought of the project as a cathartic purging of bad memories that were traumatic and never addressed at the time. Maybe by writing my story I could help other victims of sexual abuse and emotional abuse by showing them they are not alone.

Maybe I felt I was writing my story to urge other victims to seek counseling. Once in therapy, I was beginning to awaken from a bad dream, and the flashbacks of my traumatizing adolescence were becoming an everyday occurrence. I wanted to point other victims in the direction of professional counseling so that they could understand what had happened to them and begin to heal their psyches.

I wanted to reach out to other victims who were in an abusive relationship similar to mine at age thirty-seven. I thought that, through my own discoveries and healing, I could help lead the way for so many victims who were in denial—as I had been. Through my own experiences, I wanted to reach out and help others to learn how to live a better life. I wanted to give them the courage I'd found to end the pain; to recognize their own pain; and to finally say, "Enough. I have to seek help."

Once I started Al-Anon and then therapy, I began a journey I had never been on before. I never realized how many traumatic secrets I had kept locked up in my deep subconscious. I was dying inside while my husband lay on the couch drinking a beer without a care about where the rent money was coming from.

I thought of my three small children and had flashbacks of my own mother living through what I was living through now. I was determined to stop this vicious cycle. I was not going to live a life of helplessness and fear. I was going to get out of this marriage, with no regards to the future consequences!

I was afraid of my husband at the time, but I managed to get a legal separation in 1986. That lasted only six months, at which point I felt bad for him and took him back. But not long after that, his old habits of lying on the couch and not wanting to work came creeping in, and I decided then to file for a divorce. (I even stayed friends with him for thirty years till he passed away.)

After my divorce, I went back to college and got a degree in business. I had live-in students from local colleges to watch my three small sons so I could work three jobs and go to school. It paid off!

I was taking an elective course in literature called "Images of Women." I was very intrigued with what the professor was asking her students to do. She was asking each of us to give our own opinion on women who have been suppressed or abused. Her example was the women in China who were only allowed to have one baby and how these women must have felt (this rule was enacted in 1979 and was still active while I was attending college from 1986 to 1988).

I considered the point the professor was making. She wanted us to examine how we, as women, felt about sometimes having no say when it came to our bodies—whether that be because of rape, lack of abortion options, or being told how many children we were allowed to bear.

This was all relative to my question. *Why do I want to write my story?* As I started to search my memories of abuse, I started to remember one incident that I would relate to. At age fifteen, I had been a victim of a gang rape. I was raped, beaten, abused, and dropped in a field. I was left to die or fend for myself, with no idea that I was still in shock. I was a victim of abuse, who was then subsequently threatened by this gang. If I so much as uttered one word to anyone, they menaced, they would come to my house in the middle of the night and set my house on fire while my parents lay sleeping. They would find my sisters and rape them too. They told me they would be constantly watching me. I was naive and still in shock, and I believed them. They reminded me that they were a powerful gang and that no one would believe me against all of them.

They made me feel dirty and afraid. I felt that fear every day and never told anyone. Then, luckily for me, my parents decided we would move away from that town. Yet the suppressed memory of the gang rape never left my mind. It stayed close with me for many years afterwards, and it remains with me right up to the present.

I decided to write about the gang rape when our professor gave us an assignment to write about a personal experience of suppression or abuse. I chose to write about that gang rape with as much detail as I could remember and to describe how it had traumatized and affected my life for so many years. I have included in this book an entire chapter (chapter 4) that describes that horrific day back in 1965, along with the essay I wrote for this assignment.

This was no easy task. Revealing my secret and reliving that traumatic day initially made me want to just run, like I'd tried to run away that day. But through the help of my therapist and the encouragement of my professor, I managed to write in detail not only about the rape but also about how I felt about the horrendous event now and how I had felt back then on that day—the day I had never before told anyone about. My inner child had awakened, and I was finally feeling safe enough to reveal my secret of shame and guilt publicly.

I received a grade of A on that essay, along with my professor's comment that inspired and encouraged my future writings. She wrote, "It is a tribute that you, unlike so many women who have been through abuse, can so articulately voice your feelings. I am sure you can get an article out of this. The purpose is to show other women that, although the scars run deep, they can heal themselves, not alone, but through therapy, writings, family, as you have done. A powerful piece. A."

I still have that essay and read it whenever I need to bolster my courage, even after several decades have passed.

Thus the seed was planted, and the idea of this book was born. However, many years had to follow before this book would become a reality. Sexual and physical abuse was an extremely sensitive subject back in the sixties, seventies, and eighties. Even to this day, it is still a very sensitive subject. Many people do not want to talk about it, particularly if it personally affected them.

After years of revealing my multiple traumas during therapy, I realized how it had affected my youth, my adulthood, and my marriage. I began to research books related to this subject. Much to my dismay, there were not many books about sexual abuse. Back in the 1990s, I finally found a few that helped me immensely. One (which is about horrific childhood abuse but not sexual) is a book that was published in 1993 by Dave Pelzer. The title of the book is *A Child Called It*. It tells the story of a child's courage to survive his abusive childhood. It was on *The New York Times* Best Seller list for five years and sold three million copies. After reading this book, which inspired me more than I could have imagined, I began to write my story.

Now with the popularity of books of this genre, I have noticed a flood of exposure in the media, as well as on the bookshelves. This gives me hope that my book will inspire at least one person to reveal his or her fears and then deal with them by reading related subject matter books, seeking therapy, and asking family and support groups to help him or her heal. Trust me, it works!

A friend who I trusted said to me after reading this chapter, "I don't know or can imagine how you do it."

I replied, "I wasn't given a choice."

Therefore, with all my sincerity, if my book reaches and helps just one victim of abuse and inspires him or her to meet his or her full potential as I have done and then to go on and lead a better life, I have succeeded in my quest.

INTRODUCTION

Inner Silence/Inner Rage/Inner Peace

I wrote this essay when I went back to college at age thirty seven in 1986. I was going through a marital separation and hard times, yet I knew I wanted a better education in order to pursue a higher-paying job. I felt compelled to include this essay as an introduction because my professor's feedback confirmed my self-worth and belief that I was growing, not just in age but also in wisdom.

Even though it has been over thirty years since then, I always knew a bigger story was there, demanding to be completed in order to inspire other victims of abuse. I could not remain silent. I wrote this book to help other women who are victims of abuse find their own inner peace, as I have found mine. Please don't wait another moment to find your purpose and understand how powerful you really are.

June 1965

My first emotion was **confusion**. *Why is this happening to me? Why isn't anyone around, like you see on TV, the guy on the white horse? Why did they pick me? What did I do to deserve this?*

I always thought I was a good girl. I didn't flirt. I had no real boyfriends. A year before, at age fourteen, I'd already given my heart and soul away to a boy who had just laughed at me, stolen my heart, and moved away. He never saying goodbye and had left me devastated and thinking I'd never fall in love again.

I thought I had become smart. So why now? I thought that, by age fifteen, I had learned not to trust. But I was wrong.

The second emotion I felt was **guilt**. I knew I felt guilty because I had worn that bathing suit to attract attention. Well, there it is. You get what you ask for. Isn't that what we've learned? We're street smart by this time, aren't we?

Actually, I was not. I was very immature for my age. When I was fourteen I had started drinking with other kids, but I did not like it. Nor did I like smoking.

I remember getting sick on Bali Hai wine. My shame and guilt was already there—they're just clearer now in retrospect.

It might have been the crowd I hung around with too, of course. I had no close friends because my mother had to move eight times by the time I turned seventeen, due to the fact my dad was an alcoholic. He tried to work but not enough to pay the rent.

The third emotion I recognized, once I started to evaluate and relive this scene, was **fear.** I was trembling and shaking. I didn't want this gang rape to happen. I was crying, pleading, and begging.

I was scared I wasn't going to live; I was scared they were going to beat me to death. I was scared I'd never see my family again. I was scared I was going to be found dead somewhere, naked. I was also scared I'd never be able to go home again.

I never realized my sisters would have put their arms around me and told me it was going to be okay. Nor did I know then that my mother would have come home from California to help and be beside me through this ordeal and to protect me.

As for my father, well, that's another story. I wouldn't have been able to determine his reaction. Would he have accused me of asking for it, of giving it away? This was what I thought his reaction might be.

In my head, this was a life-threatening event. I had every reason to be scared and confused.

The last emotion I felt, until therapy, was **sadness.** I cried myself to sleep that day. I kept it all inside to mask the anger I should have been able to express.

From this sadness evolved a clown-like girl, always hiding her real sadness—the sadness she felt when she closed her door at night, when she shut the lights off, and when she was alone driving in her car. She would take lonely walks, sadness always by her side. Sadness was her friend, her companion, for many years.

No one knew this sad person. They only saw what she wanted them to see. She told jokes and made up stories. She took care of everyone else's problems. She would argue for everyone else but not for herself. She made sure she kept busy. She would work two to three jobs at a time. She had become so independent after the rape that she did not have time to think. She would do this through more painful times after the first rape. She faced the hardest times all alone. Her secrets are still hers.

She kept her secrets for many years, but now they are being revealed during counseling. For the first time, she actually feels safe, able to speak, to express, and to feel. She can pull back her secrets any time she wants to in therapy. She can let some of them out and let them go now because of therapy. She can actually be normal and experience the real feelings most people take for granted in a good, nurturing, healthy family life.

I feel envious when I see how healthy other people's lives are, but I am glad I am able to feel that jealousy and to learn and grow from it. I can do this for my own children now. I can protect them. I can now lay there and play a healthy tickling game, where years ago I would never have allowed them to play at tickling or in any other intimately fun games. Where did I learn that? Well, I was living in a bubble for too long, and it just popped! I can happily say I am the one who popped it. I have become free.

I hope I have made some sense to someone out there who has experienced any type of trauma or abuse. If that person is you, I hope you seek some sort of help. We all need an outlet to vent our anger. We need to trust and to let go, to be guided. We need help. We are victims who have been pulled down, intimidated, and abused. We must not succumb to the events that we have experienced. We must fight for ourselves and for our sanity.

No one knows what's going on in our heads except other victims. We must be able to scream, to rage, and to be silent no more! These words are a list I compiled while brainstorming one afternoon. If you feel you have a hard time with any one of these words, then stop, examine the word, close your eyes, and let the word take you wherever it wants to go. You've just begun.

Guilt

Suffering

Acceptance

Contacting

Talking

Confiding

Trusting

Relating

Limited

Confused

Users

Sad

Serious

Vulnerable

Scared

Silent

Rage

Victims

Abused

Anger

If anyone thinks rape only happens to girls or women who may have provoked it, then I feel sorry for his or her lack of understanding. It can and does happen to anyone, of any age, in any sector of society—sometimes more than once. Take that from me; I have been there. It has such an impact that all one can do to survive is to try and erase or suppress the memory. We can stuff it down, or we can reach out. It is just too painful to relive or look at and deal with alone.

My survival depended on my ability to hide and suppress my pain. We are so unaware of the anger and grief we have suppressed. We are totally unaware of our choices now and of our rights. The effects rape has on your womanhood or your own mothering are hard to discern. Think of how angry you get and how you can't figure out why you are so angry or sad. Think of how, one day, you wake up from this secret and try to understand it. You know the experience has left horrible marks on you mentally. You struggle not to feel ashamed and to tell yourself everything is okay. It is not okay! Get rid of this guilt before it cripples you. No one has the right to hurt you or take from you what you are not willing to give.

If you've kept your secrets inside and feel it's not worth revealing them, take a look around you and see what is true. Is your world safe and sound? Are you a trusting person? Do you feel fairly secure? Do you have a nice job? A nice mate? A nice home?

Do your children behave "normally"? How's your self-esteem? Do you take the last piece of cold chicken from the plate at suppertime when everyone else is already done eating? How well do you respond to the lifestyles of today that surround you? How do you respond to sex? To rape? To incest? To disease? To abortion?

These are all issues that are part of our everyday lives; they have to affect you and your life. There is no time clock saying you must get those secrets out of the closet, deal with them, and remember what you learned from them. No, the clock is not saying this; the time bomb was set a long time ago. It's time to *diffuse* it!

CHAPTER 1

Denial

How did this happen? Why was I the one sitting in this old—and I mean very old—house that used to be a home to someone back in the early 1800s? According to a plaque on the front door, the house was built in 1801 and was now a facility called "Family Counseling." But to me it looked so dull and dim that I couldn't wait to get out of there.

Why was I here? A friend of mine, who I admired for her courage to admit that her own life was in turmoil—something no one knew or would have guessed—encouraged me to try counseling therapy. "Just go try it," she said. "And then you will see how my life turned around. I went from an abusive marriage to solutions that I am happy with now."

This old house, now called Family Counseling, is a facility where people may come for help with whatever their problems might be.

Some people don't even realize they are not living life to its fullest and enjoying a healthy, rewarding life. They are not cognizant of the dysfunctions of their lives and try to cope with their feeling that something is basically wrong, while remaining silent. Why should they go to a strange place when they felt certain they have no need to go? For me, going to therapy was a last resort—a last attempt to try and save my marriage. That was my intent, not my husband's, because he thought nothing was wrong with our marriage. Neither he nor I had ever gone to a professional therapist before, but here we were.

I was sitting in an office and staring at two old, tiny doors. Maybe they were like prison doors, longing to be opened. Maybe opening them would release me from the bondage I did not even fully know I was in—the chains I had kept so safely hidden for all those years in my own inner silence and rage.

At age thirty-six, after having been married for nine years, I wanted a separation from my husband. His drinking was getting out of control and his verbal, physical, and sexual behavior was getting too aggressive. After my second child was born, I tried hard to avoid my feelings, which were that I did not want sex anymore. It was a progressive feeling. There were no conscious emotions that I felt, just a void in my life. I had no desire for any man, really, and never entertained that idea. I just wanted to be left alone. I wanted to be mommy, not wife.

I would make excuses not to have sex. I would clean and polish the floor on my hands and knees at night just to avoid going to bed before he did. Luck had it that he had to get up at 5:00 a.m., so I would wait until he fell asleep before I crept into our bed or my children's beds.

The marriage was crumbling, and I never realized how bad it was until undergoing therapy. I was the one who wanted to try to fix it, to start this marriage counseling. Reluctantly, he agreed to do this for me. He had no clue what was going on in my mind, and neither did I.

So I made the appointment. This facility was dark inside. And there were fireplaces, it seemed, in every room—tiny, dimly lit rooms that still exuded an aura from the time the facility was built. Narrow stairs and hallways connected the various parts of the building. Several stairways actually went up the front and down the back of this old house. Old wallpaper, dark draped curtains, towering old glass pane windows; and wide wooden panel floors were in every room.

I was imagining the kind of people who'd formerly walked around, like ghosts holding candles, as they flowed in and out of the rooms in an ethereal way. It was creepy to me at first, all the actual walking around above this office room I was sitting in. The creaking floors made you aware that someone else was walking around upstairs. I guess I felt more curious than I felt afraid, in that room. It was like a movie to me, and I was letting my imagination get away from me.

Most of all, it was the closet in that room that caught my attention. It was the latch, different from any latch I'd ever seen, and the hinges, which were in the shape of old swords, only placed sideways, and unusually bigger than anything that belonged to a normal house door that first caught my attention. Maybe they were from the nearby prison back in former days, I thought.

Then there was the skeleton keyhole that most captured my gaze. It was larger than a normal keyhole, like the ones you would see in a castle. I thought, *Could there be someone peeking out at me from in there?* Or was the impression symbolic of me inside my own mind, peeking and trying to get out?

I wondered how long this interview would take before I could leave. Then my husband would have to stay, as I had thought beforehand. Surely they could counsel him about his aggressiveness and attitude, so we could at least try to save our marriage for our children.

I kept thinking about this place, instead of our problem. I wondered how many sane people came in and out of here. Not many, I imagined. But then again, I was compelled to set the record straight. I had no problems. It was my husband who had the problem, which was his obsession with controlling me, in and out of bed.

I didn't let this old house or the people or the haunting ghosts that were there in my imagination, longing to be let out, get to me.

Ironically it was the beginning of the New England fall season, a cold, windy, and spooky night in October, precisely at 7:00 p.m., and almost Halloween time. That probably explains my feelings. That night of our first appointment has been burned into the corners of my mind and remains to this day. Little did I know that it was the beginning of a long and bittersweet journey for me! I had no clue what was about to transpire on this night.

Our first session was with a tall, stern-looking woman who happened to be the intake counselor. She introduced herself and started asking

3

questions about why we were there and how they could help us. I explained that I had lost my desire for sex with my husband.

"How long ago did this start?" she asked me. "Are you in any danger or distress?"

How did she know?

Of course, I was not so quick to answer, and it seemed to me that she was focusing all the questions on me, when I thought she should be focusing on him. *It's not me!* I was getting irritated, as was my husband. He was shifting, fidgeting, and clearing his throat and ready to explode. I could feel it. He was getting ready to snap, as he had frequently done with me in the past. I thought we would be thrown out.

Then she turned to my husband and basically asked the same questions that she had asked me. This gave him the chance to say that the issues were my fault—that I was just going through some silly emotional phase and that we could work this out privately. He was arrogant and obnoxious. His male ego was not to be tampered with.

He told her this was all a big mistake, and he felt that I would snap out of it eventually.

The nerve of him, I thought to myself. *I can't believe how he just turned the situation all around!* I sensed at that moment the counselor knew he was not going to cooperate or attend any more meetings.

She asked my husband if she could talk with me alone. I could tell she found my husband to be arrogant. I guessed he figured she would talk some sense into me, so he agreed. And I agreed I would speak with her alone. He was ushered into another room, where there was another counselor, and the door was shut. He never spoke about what went on or what was said while he was in that other room.

She asked me about my husband. "Do you feel frightened or threatened by him?"

I sat there silently, thinking my answer was, *Yes. He intimidates me constantly.* But I didn't say a word.

She asked me if I'd experienced any traumas recently or as a child. A flash of me being gang raped at age fifteen came flooding into my mind and across my saddened face. She was observing my pain and my delayed reaction, and how, when I responded to her questions, I showed no emotion. No, that wasn't unusual. It had always been easier for me to hide my multiple traumas or better still, keep silent about them and bury them deep within my mind. This was when my inner silence/inner rage began to surface. How could this be happening?

After a few more questions regarding the rape and some of my marriage history, she told me I could begin counseling immediately! I was completely in shock, astonished, bewildered, and embarrassed!

I said to myself, *Wait just a minute here. What do you mean I can start therapy? He's the one with the problems, certainly not me!* I was the one who made our pretty white house with the white picket fence. It was my labor of love, along with my beautiful rock garden and flowering pink dogwood tree. I was the best mom in the whole town. I was the lunch mom, the soccer mom, the library mom, the Boy Scout mom. I even had cloth diapers and a clothesline in my backyard, and this was in the 1980s, when mothers were buying Pampers and using clothes driers.

I made brownies. I sewed my children's outfits. I went to tailoring classes and woodworking classes, taught religion classes, and read stories to my three little boys every night. I took them to their baseball games, their soccer games, and their Boy Scout events. I arranged museum visits and family outings and attended every school event, while my husband *never* participated in any one of our children's academic activities or in our family life. I had the cleanest house, with pretty hand-stenciled walls and beautiful pictures of the perfect family I was trying to hold together. How dare he say to her that I had the problem?

My husband met me out front having his cigarette and telling me I was stupid. I guess that's what made me call back the next day for an appointment.

CHAPTER 2

Acceptance

Here I was in 1986, thirty-seven years old and going through a major meltdown in my life. But on a more positive note, I had entered a different chapter of my life then. This time, I had entered a place in which I had started to feel safe. I was attending therapy group sessions and in the care of my very capable therapist. I had just started opening some of my inner closet doors that had been closed for over thirty years.

I had started my therapy and felt confident I could deal with my healing, while also reaching out to other victims of abuse. I had been diagnosed with PTSD, bipolarity, manic depression, anxiety symptoms, and ADD. However, I felt I could overcome the negative effects of these various disorders through my strong faith in God, together with my therapy and refusal of any drugs.

My story is based on the blueprint of my life before and during marriage. It consists of several major traumas, including rape, abandonment, and abuse in every possible way—emotional, physical, mental, and sexual. I was living a completely dysfunctional life, totally unaware of my own unhappiness. I had grown accustomed to living in a bubble, never letting myself cry or feel anything, never letting my guard down.

I feel that now, talking and writing about my traumas, along with undergoing therapy, I can manage each day a little better, one day at a time. Writing this book is therapy for me. It allows me to open the closet doors in my mind and helps me in my recovery. And hopefully, it will help other victims of abuse as well.

I had managed to project an image of an ordinary, reasonably "normal" teenage girl who grew up to be a loving mother and wife. No one would ever guess such a woman had a multitude of hidden issues for so many years.

I started to write my story to help others find *their* inner child and begin their healing. My focus in this book is on three rapes and the repercussions of a dysfunctional marriage. I'll reveal how I eventually became a raging woman—once I started my meltdown—many years later.

The fact that I can write calmly about this today is evidence that self-help books, therapy, various classes, and time can all contribute to the healing process. Time is the healer, so it's said, so let's not let time slip away without taking affirmative action.

I was raised, as previously noted, by my Catholic mother and an alcoholic father. My mother was very close to her parents and relied on them a lot because my father's drinking made him totally useless. Her father died the year before I was born, which devastated her. Then her mother died when I was less than a year old. My mother had so much pain, but she mustered up enough strength and faith to get her and us through the many tough times that lay ahead.

As I think back in time and because I wish to respect their privacy, I do not feel it appropriate for me to discuss any of my family's lives, as we each have our own thoughts. This book is solely about me and my own issues. It's about how, as I grew up, I kept everything from them, telling no one about the pain inflicted on me and the suffering I was enduring.

I have written about several specific traumas in the following chapters. These traumas are very shocking, but the details need to be told in order for you, my reader, to understand what I had been through prior to seeking therapy. They are true events and were very hard for me to write about, but they were my metaphorical DNA and will help the reader to see how far I have grown.

This story is written to try and reach as many people as possible. My hope is to enable others to recognize the traumas resulting from or the signs of abuse that they or someone else they're close to or in contact with may have experienced or be experiencing now.

Never did I expect that therapy would reveal to me how much I had concealed. I had not been aware, prior to my therapy, on a conscious level that these things had happened. Nor could I clearly see the damage they had done to me, preventing me from having a normal adolescent life, healthy self-esteem, and fulfillment.

My parents moved eight times before I turned seventeen, leaving me with no significant memories of childhood friends, just memories of each of the houses. My entire childhood was an emotional roller coaster ride. My father worked odd jobs here and there, as a painter or wallpaper hanger, but the money he brought in from these endeavors didn't pay the rent or cover all the bills. Strangely enough, he was considered a likeable man by many, but he was an alcoholic just the same.

Once you read about all the things that happened to me, you're going to ask yourself, how did she get through it all? How could she forget? As I look back now, I had to ask myself that very same question over and over. All I can say is I had no choice. That's why I'm writing this book. I want to help others who have been sexually, mentally, verbally, physically, or emotionally abused. Abuse comes in many different forms, but they all usually result in traumas that you need not go through alone—not now or ever again.

You see, you never really forget. You just file all of it away in the back of your mind, where it is hidden and safe. You feel guilt and shame but don't address it or talk about it, because you have mastered your subconscious mind without even knowing it. This is so you won't traumatize yourself over and over. Then, through therapy, you learn about acceptance. And after acceptance, you learn how to go about building self-esteem and then fulfillment. What will you accept now? Do you want to keep on denying your past abuse? Or do you want to consciously accept it so you can heal?

All of the experiences I had encountered with life up to the point of this writing had been put away—which had protected me from ever getting mentally depressed or weak.

Before starting therapy I had a strong tendency to run from any confrontation, but during therapy I worked diligently to get rid of that tendency. I would love to sit down and evaluate why I did that, but there are so many traumatic events in my mind that it would be overwhelming to recall them all. For instance, all three rapes that I focus on here in this account happened within a three-year span.

When your psyche opts to tune traumatic experiences out, you are totally unaware of your avoidance. You don't even know you're avoiding the experiences that traumatized you. Instead, you mask what lies beneath. For example, I would disguise my feelings by adopting a funny clown façade, while deep inside, I was aching to shed my disguise and end the masquerade.

I had spent the whole day yesterday trying to write some part of this manuscript, but I found myself procrastinating, eating a peanut butter fluff sandwich with lots of marshmallow on it. I could only write about two pages and would have to stop. Even this morning, when I woke up, I felt exhausted. I didn't want to write, I didn't want to get out of my pajamas, I didn't want to get out of bed, and I didn't want to go to Sunday Mass. I was making up excuses to myself, promising that I would do everything that night or tomorrow. These are the signs that tell me I am trying to rest my inner child after a bad memory that has surfaced.

It's not as if you can just sit down and pull all the memories up that have been lying dormant in your mind for years. All will eventually surface but not until you feel safe enough to put them in writing. I recognized the signs—eat and push your memories back down into your subconscious. The day had been a gorgeous, sunny, warm New England Fall day, but I didn't want to leave my room. I just stayed in all day long because it was safe, and I could sleep and forget the emotions that were raging inside me caused by the trigger I call writing.

These days are what I call triggers. It could be a smell, a sound, a voice, a movie, a person or a taste, anything that suddenly causes a bad memory to surface. I kept lying down on my bed just waiting for nightfall so I could go to sleep, but it wouldn't pass. I just tossed and turned all night long.

The books and articles I read throughout my recovery consisted of inspirational, real-life stories written for the purpose of self-help. These accounts helped me to survive all the new experiences I was encountering. That's another reason I'm writing this book—that it may find its way to others like me, who are facing their own traumas. I want to help them, guide them, and pray for their recovery.

I am changing now. I recognize myself getting stronger and more self-reliant. I feel the urge to write this book with power, strength, and energy, as opposed to how I felt in the beginning—totally exhausted after a session with the counselor or after remembering something I'd written in the past. Now it was time to feel the anger, the emotions, and the pain in full force, so I could move on with a more fulfilling life, understanding that the traumas in my past were not my fault.

I am writing here some notes that I compiled in the past twenty odd years. Of course, all my notes are scrambled as a result of the many traumas I experienced and the numerous houses I've lived in. Once I smelled, heard, or tasted something that brought me back to a bad time, I would stop and write it down. Then I had to sort out which year it occurred in or how old I was when it happened or what house was involved. And I remembered. As confusing as it could be, I still remembered. I am so grateful for having such a brilliant memory, but sometimes it's a curse.

I gathered the courage and took a leap of faith; I opened my mind and my memories. Sometimes the recollections emerge, but sometimes they don't, which leaves me totally frustrated. I stay focused and wait patiently for an answer to a problem that has not been resolved, knowing it will come in its own due time or not at all.

Don't get me wrong. I still have my setbacks, and I still see my therapist, because re-traumatizing yourself requires someone to be there for you—someone who can help and guide you.

I have my memories, and whether I wanted them to emerge or not, they were coming. This was because I had made those first steps toward a new life—toward healing. I'd started therapy classes. I'd joined Al-Anon. Even enrolling in college was a step. My therapy, which I call "divine intervention" (see chapter 3), was my salvation. I was not going to let my mind stagnate or forget all the rotten, horrific traumatic things that I had experienced in my adolescence and beyond and had suppressed all these years. I needed to heal and build up my self-esteem and self-worth.

I would have ended up a drug addict, an alcoholic, a manic-depressive, or suffering a destructive personality disorder. But I kept reading my self-help and inspirational books to ward off my demons. These books helped me to cope, to understand, and to survive the hell I was going through and led me to a higher knowing that I was worthy of the best in life. To this very day, as I write my story, I read books all the time. And when I know someone else is having a hard time, I know exactly what book to give each person that would help him or her.

You need to feel safe and secure in order to write about something like this. You also need to be serious about helping others like yourself. And you have to have a strong faith, because that is what gives you the courage to go on. If you read the Bible, you will see that Jesus teaches us that we're all connected. It's just aligning yourself with the positive people that will help you on your journey of healing. It's what I call "networking."

Sometimes I am in disbelief of all of the things that happened to me. I ask myself, *Did that really happen to me?* You automatically doubt your recollection of events because you were so traumatized before. Once you feel a little safer to come forward, you still get that 1 percent doubt. This has always been my weakness. I'm always second-guessing myself.

I never took drugs, ever. As I got older, I hated the idea that I wouldn't be aware of what would happen to me if I allowed myself to be under the influence of drugs or let my guard down and got high or low, with a resultant loss of control. I guess that was what I learned early on; that was my "safe mode" mechanism. Always trying to read other people's minds—a survival technique—helped me be aware of my surroundings and circumstances.

All of this reflects back to the experiences I went through and the traumas I encountered while growing up. I would take my mind out of the moment when I was being sexually abused or otherwise traumatized. As I grew older, I could handle whatever came to me because I had mastered and controlled all of my thoughts. At least I felt I had. My body was there in that moment, but not my mind.

I now had a chance to examine all the events and experiences that I'd suppressed. Now this day was here, the first of many days where my mind could feel calm, and I would let those awful memories and events emerge from my subconscious. I would let them be unveiled and let my inner child heal and help other children in the process.

My story is written with a strong desire from me to you, my reader, in hopes that you do not wait for these emotions to surface later in your life, as they did in mine, so many years ago, wasting so much precious time. It's your turn now to take care of yourself.

I could finally address acceptance. But that's not where it all stops. That concept, *acceptance*, was just a tiny fraction of what and who I really was becoming. In therapy, I have just begun and have a long road ahead of me. My sincere wish is that I bring someone out there the courage and tenacity to never give up.

I've always hoped that, one day, I will truly know who I am and why I'm here. I desire to know the purpose of my life. And I say that, my reader, to assure you—that you are not alone.

This book is written with sincerity and not to bring attention to me. It is written with honesty. And I've shared my recollections with clarity to shed light on the traumas that I've personally gone through and about which I've kept silent. Never did I ever expect that the words of one friend, "Just go check out this therapist," would change my life forever.

CHAPTER 3

Divine Intervention

I know how strange it feels that I have accepted silently and kept hidden all these traumas and abuse. Yet I live and breathe as normally as normal can be to have survived and to tell about it. What has kept me going is a strong faith in God. I knew He was there somewhere telling me this was my story and that I had to share it in order to help others.

I understand that other victims do not have faith or cannot apply their faith to what has happened to them. But we all need to trust at some point in our life. I chose God because there was no other person in my conscious mind that I could trust. I also know that it's not just God that a victim needs in order to trust. But if you're reading this book, please trust me as a victim myself that you need to take the leap of faith in order to start dealing with your inner child.

I used to make up poems and songs when I was younger, and I still have them today. I wrote about nature a lot—about the seasons and about animals. I even wrote one poem to my father and one to my mother. But most of all, I wrote about love. I depicted the love that hurts, the love that cries, the love that is unmet, the love I never had, and the love that needs. I was missing that one piece of the puzzle in life that is called *love*, and my poems portrayed a lonely girl.

I had no idea that there was anything bad in my past that made me who I was becoming. I was aware of the rapes and aware of my fears, but damn that was nothing because I had mastered *denial*, *acceptance*, and *silence*! These were the keys to my closet, where everything "unsavory" went.

I started counseling reluctantly. And after my first session of therapy, I began my journey of opening the closet that was in that counselor's room. That was the only way I could describe it back then. I would sit there many times and stare at that closet, wondering how many hearts that had been torn apart were in that closet. How many had come out of it and survived? I would ask myself. How many tears had been shed in this room? How many denials were insisted on, how many conquests were addressed right here in this room, in this facility known as Family Counseling.

To this day, I do believe that, if I had not gotten there to the therapist when I did, I would have fallen into a deep depression. I would likely have lost myself, because that was where I was heading.

I had my work cut out for me; it was so hard in the beginning. I would find all sorts of excuses not to go there. I would break appointments, I would cancel appointments, and I would lie about why I didn't go. I would sleep and forget an appointment. But the thing that I most clearly recognized after leaving those sessions was that I would get terribly cold. It didn't matter if I had on a sweater, coat, or just a summer outfit. I would leave completely chilled—the kind of cold that gets down to your bones and you're so freezing cold that you need a blanket or something warm (or maybe, possibly a hug) right away.

I told my therapist about these moments, and she asked me what I thought of it. As I sat there, for the first time in my life, I began to ask myself some questions—something I'd seemingly never done before. I came to the conclusion that, whenever I was feeling cold after a session, it was because I was hitting a nerve, a trauma, or an unpleasant memory.

I use to walk to Family Counseling, and even on a hot summer's day, I would be freezing on the way home, just thinking over what we'd talked about for that one hour, once a week on Mondays.

I would go home after my session, alone once more, home to my three little cherubs who my mother-in-law would be babysitting for me, as she lived downstairs in our house and loved watching my three little boys.

I would never think to tell my mother-in-law what my past was about or what I had been through because I was not quite sure how to deal with it myself. But she did adore me and never asked me questions about my therapy.

Before therapy, I was never sure of myself. Even if I were 99 percent sure of something, there remained that 1 percent that would cause me self-doubt. I would never be sure or dare to debate my own questions.

I remember my first visit to this place called Family Counseling and the woman who was assigned me to. I didn't like her right away. But then again, it must have been me, right? I was the one with the problems that I had no clue I had. I was in major denial.

I cried the first session and walked home, vowing never to return to that place ever again. Hell, my husband would have been happy if I'd stopped. He didn't know any of my story or life back then, and he never asked. He just wanted his wife back; he just wanted things to return to the way they used to be—back when I was living in a dream.

But something was wrong, and the timing was right. There would be no more secrets, no more avoidance, no more pretending that everything was fine, because it wasn't fine anymore. Something was missing in this so-called dream of mine. I wasn't sleeping, or I was sleeping too much.

My mother was over one day visiting and babysitting. She was doing a puzzle on the dining room table, and I was lying on the couch, soaking in the warmth of the sun shining through my big bow window. Then the phone rang, I let it ring a bit and finally answered it. (We did not have caller ID back then). It was the counselor or therapist, whichever.

The counselor said, "We had an appointment today. Is something wrong?"

I got mad and said, "No. I just forgot." She insisted on me coming the following week, and I said, "Okay."

My mother was up babysitting and doing her jigsaw puzzle and asked, "Who that was on the phone?"

"That crazy counselor I went to down the street," I told her. "She thinks it's me with the problems, not him!"

I'll never forget my mother's *icy* reaction. She just bowed her head back down to her puzzle and said, "I see." Those two words were a breakthrough for me. It was as if she was saying it was okay to go there—that she understood and it was okay and that, yes, there was something wrong with me.

You see, I was beginning to sleep too much and would ask my mother to come over (and she did live far away) to watch the kids while I slept. The other me—who was full of energy; never stopping; always go, go, go—had left. And here emerged this washed-out, drained, pathetic human being with manic tendencies, now lying and sleeping on the couch.

And so I brought myself to call and make the appointment. When I got there, I was told that the other counselor had left. *Good*, I thought to myself. *But who'll be next on my list of therapists that I hate?*

Instead I was introduced to Anne. We hit it off right away. Anne was this kind, soft-spoken, refined elderly lady who was so concerned for me. She had beautiful white hair and dressed very conservatively. She always wore a skirt, a silk blouse, a jacket, and her strand of pearls. It was all about me now, and she guided and coached me that way. She admired me and would tell me so, but I was the one who admired her more.

Her office room was in the back of the facility where the sun would come in most of the day. The front of this facility was covered with thick trees, which grew around the windows of the room where I'd had my previous meetings with the other counselor, making very dark inside that room. I was very glad that Anne's office was in the back of the building—on the sunny side. I was in enough darkness in my life.

I loved the sun coming in to warm me in this room. She had plants all around the room, and I loved plants. I had tons of them in my own home too. The room was very bright and cheery, which would put you in a different frame of mind than did the dark meeting room of the other therapist—the room where I had begun this journey.

When I talked, Anne would listen attentively. Whenever she asked me a question, it was in such a manner that I never felt threatened. Anne knew things about me that were preventing me from releasing my demons. For example, she knew the guilt, shame, and pain I was desperately trying so hard to hide.

I remember one time Anne asked me to list on one side of a piece of paper all the good things I found myself to be. And on the other side, I was to list all the not so good things I found myself to be. She said, 'I bet you find more good than bad." I was supposed to do this at home, during the week prior to our next session.

I told her I couldn't think of anything good. I could only list things related to my bad side—my sleeping so much and what not.

She gave me some good things to ponder on. She mentioned how I loved to write poems and loved to read to my kids. She pointed out my beautiful curly hair and pretty blue eyes. Shouldn't I think those were good things to ponder on?

Well, I got to thinking all that week and kept adding to the good list.

Now keep in mind that I had no positive self-esteem or self-confidence. I was always waiting for the other shoe to drop or a fight to break out because of my childhood traumas. I used to think, if you drew attention to yourself, you would attract the wrong impression. Because of the guilt I felt related to the rapes, I would tell myself not to try and look pretty or to even consider myself as attractive. My focus was family and home and making sure everyone else was happy. It took a long time for me to feel good about myself, a very long time.

I did have lots of love to give out without ever finding or expecting love in return. Anne knew how to build my self-esteem, and I couldn't wait for our next session. She would even coach me into going to other classes that were available at this facility and that were offered practically for free. One class I took was entitled "Becoming More Assertive." The next class was "Self-Esteem," and another was "Your Creative Self." You name it. I did it.

Then there was this one class I did not want to take. But Anne coached me into it, reassuring me that I could get out of it if it proved too hard for me to handle. So I did. It was called "Rape and Sexual Abuse." This was the most important one for me to go to. It would help me deal with all the issues I may have been harboring in my mind about the three rapes and would help me to see that I was not alone in dealing with this type of trauma.

The "Rape and Sexual Abuse" class was about the hardest for me out of all the classes I ever took at this facility. My old patterns of sleeping or finding excuses not to go to the class kept creeping in. I sat there at the first class trembling in fear as those gathered in a circle—about six women and two therapists—shared one by one. I couldn't believe my ears when these women would tell their story and the sexual abuse they'd endured.

I was in shock. I was numb. And I felt bad for the women, not knowing at that moment that it was my own inner child who was hurting.

When it was my turn to talk about my "beginning" or my awareness of what had happened to me, I was calm and told them, "I was gang-raped at fifteen years old." I did not elaborate any details and became silent. But what was nice about this group was that it was okay. The therapist knew that, in due time, I would have my peace.

There were grave stories in that room. I missed the second class on purpose. I couldn't go back and listen to those poor women cry and hurt. I wasn't thinking at the time that it was me who didn't want to cry and who didn't want to think or talk about the pain I'd experienced. I had been conditioned never to talk—to keep the abuse I'd endured a secret. *You'll be punished if you tell.* This was the message I'd been told and had integrated. *There will be hell to pay. And besides, no one will believe you. You're a liar. You're just a kid making trouble.* Or better still, *You asked for it.* I was guilty for turning the boys who raped me on.

After the first class, I needed someone right that minute to talk with, and Anne was always there. All I had to do was call, and she would get back to me. I felt insecure and confused. I wanted to run, to avoid this mess. Yet now I was driven to it, into the eye of it. Where did it begin? How far back did I go? Where was I during the blackout times? And were they important?

Sometimes I really thought I had a good childhood, and other times, I thought not. There was no consistency in my feelings. Why did I care? How could I let go? What was I looking for? How would I know? Could I let it go?

And now, do I think I will be able to let go once the book is finished? I know now that the trauma I experienced will never be totally gone from my thoughts. A smell alone can trigger an experience. But I do feel that letting go to the extent I can do so will allow me to feel free and to move on with a lighter heart while helping others. I certainly hope so.

Although the purpose of this book is to help others, I can attest that things do get better over time and that exposing and dealing with the traumas you've faced is certainly therapeutic. This book will be my guidebook for you. And hopefully it will inspire you to take steps toward healing.

If any of you, my readers doesn't have faith that it will get better, I strongly urge you to start asking yourself some questions and to find your Source, your comfort, and your safety zone. Call your therapist, call a sibling who loves and understands you, and call your best friend. I personally find peace and answers to a problem when I'm outside in nature, walking the pond, hiking a trail, walking along the ocean edge, or sitting under a tree in a quiet place and closing my eyes. Then, without my knowing, answers begin to gently come forward.

The memories that you carry through your entire life may be obscured, hidden, and unclear. Yet one day, you will wake up from this nightmare. And as hard as it may seem now, you will face it, or you will never be free. I reached out without even knowing to a counselor who knew my story before I knew where I had been, what I had seen, and what I had encountered.

The great part of all this is one thing. *You* survived. You have a story. And the rest—how you deal with it—is up to you. You have choices now. Tell your story, share it, ask for help, get help, and find a professional. Help is the reason I am here telling you these things.

My relationship with Anne and the counseling facility where I found her lasted about ten years. And during that time, I took no medicines. The facility shut down due to lack of funding. I must say the journey was bittersweet. I bet if it were not for Anne, I wouldn't have a memory of my past anymore. I'd be numb, possibly manic-depressive, and depending on drugs for the rest of my life, never remembering and not feeling anything.

So that's it. Trust was what I lacked as I started off on this new journey. It was a gift that Anne gave to me. I look back with such love for her, and I credit her with saving my life.

Today I do feel good most of the time. But I'm getting ahead of myself.

Let's go back now a couple of decades to give you a better understanding of the actual events and the traumas I had endured before I started therapy; before opening up; and, most of all, before I could trust anyone to share my past and my healing journey with.

CHAPTER 4

The Quarries Gang Rape

This chapter is the hardest for me to write, as the events I'll share here took place at a time when I was beginning to know myself better than ever before. My parents had just moved again, and I was still adjusting. I was so excited that I would finally be going onto high school in September. That was very important to me because I would be seeing the same friends from the eighth grade, and we were now going into the ninth grade together.

Age fifteen was a tender and special time for me. I could laugh at silly things, have a best friend or friends, and feel like I wasn't a little girl anymore. I was finally feeling like a teenager. I was more conscious and aware of myself and who I chose to hang around with. I was never a follower. I just picked and chose my friends and knew who not to trust. I was very intuitive for my age—or so I thought. My downfall was that I cared too much for others—more than I cared for myself.

I knew that I could chose to make an impression or a statement, and I would now fit in. I no longer wanted to be that introverted, uninformed, naive young girl I had been the year before. I was done being the young girl who had all the cares in the world and who'd kept to herself for so long. This chapter is about me letting my guard down and trying to fit in.

I was not a shapely girl and felt all the other girls were more mature-looking than me. I was sort of shy and flat-chested. I didn't even wear a bra yet. I was extremely skinny, opposed to all the girls in the group, and felt confused, as I was different.

I only had one close girlfriend, whose name was Anne Marie. All the rest were just classmate acquaintances. Anne Marie and I lived just about five (what we called) blocks away or a bus ride away from each other and managed to see each other as often as we could in school or after school. I used to take the bus over to her house for sleepovers. Her parents were divorced, so it was just her mom who would watch over us while we played records and danced and laughed and sang. I never had friends over to my house because my father would usually be home sleeping, so we couldn't make much noise.

This particular incident happened on a beautiful, bright sunny day in June. Anne Marie and I were so excited because we would be graduating from the eighth grade and heading on to the ninth grade. We felt like we had just won a million dollars. We would be walking across the school stage receiving our junior high school diplomas (which I still have). And we were both going to be going to the same high school that following September, which made it even more special. I finally had a long-term friend—or so I thought.

That day, the entire eighth grade class had to practice walking across the stage to get our diplomas. We would be released from school early after practice. We got out early from the rest of the classes! How special was that for two fifteen-year-old teenagers.

Anne Marie and I, along with a bunch of the other eighth graders, decided to walk to the square and get an ice cream shake at the ice cream parlor. Anne Marie was an extremely beautiful girl, and nothing seemed to scare her. She would tell other kids to buzz off, or when she knew she was right, she would argue until she won her point. She was great at sports, unlike me. I always felt I had two left feet and would not participate in sports or any other physically challenging activity.

As we were on our way to the ice cream parlor, there were two boys in a car, parked right in front of us as were walking. One of the boys had a crush on Anne Marie, and she had a crush on him. I don't know how she knew him. Maybe he lived in her neighborhood, but she had never mentioned him to me before. I think he was sixteen or seventeen.

The two boys got out of the car and started talking to us. We were getting a lot of attention from the other kids because Anne Marie and I were now ninth graders, and these boys were going into the eleventh grade, and they had a car.

Looking at these boys, I thought to myself, *Let's get out of here now.* But I didn't want to hurt Anne Marie's feelings. I knew she liked the boy because she told me she did when they were approaching us. This boy she liked was Matt. His friend looked like a creep to me and acted like a creep. He had that black, greasy, slicked-back hair and a pack of cigarettes in his T-shirt sleeve like something out of the movie *Grease*. He had rotten teeth, and his clothes looked too tight. When he talked, he sounded like a gangster. He really thought he was something else, and that was a turnoff for me. I started to feel apprehensive and was waiting for the other shoe to drop, as I always do when I feel an uneasy encounter developing. At fifteen years old, I was intuitive and could read people very well. I should not have been thinking about Anne Marie. I should have been thinking of my feelings. This was one guy I did not want to meet or associate with!

After Anne Marie had spent a great amount of time talking with Matt while I stood there frowning in disapproval, I finally spoke up and told Anne Marie that I wanted to go home. She thought I had lost my mind! She'd just told me how much she'd been dying to meet up with this boy.

That was when they suggested we go to the nearby quarries with them to go swimming and to celebrate our graduation. I said I didn't want to go. But Anne Marie was very persuasive when she wanted to have her way, so I reluctantly agreed to go. I could say no (my gut feeling was urging me to do so, and I should have listened) and have my one and only best friend not talk to me ever again. Or I could say yes and just keep to myself (or so I thought). I had no idea that the quarries were a haven for boys and nude swimming. I should have been more informed.

I finally spoke up and said that we had no bathing suits.

Anne Marie replied cheerfully, "We can go to your house and get some bathing suits from your sisters. They won't be home, and your dad won't bother you because I'll be there with you." She had that look on her face that said, *Don't you dare screw this up for me.* So I reluctantly agreed to go back to my house to get our bathing suits and towels.

My mother, at the time, was in California, visiting my brother and sister. That left my father home alone and probably drunk when I got out of school every day. I hated being around him when he was drinking.

I didn't know how to swim at the time. I was just a city kid, and no one around where I lived had swimming pools. Once in a while, we were taken to the YMCA, where there was a pool and swimming instructors. But I never took lessons. Consequently, I didn't know how to swim. But it didn't matter to the two boys. They said there were plenty of rocks to sit on where you could dangle your feet in the cool water. Plus, the water at the quarries was from a spring and had many pools to play in. They also explained that there were lots of shallow pools to wade in, which was a lie.

I told the boys to meet us around the block so my dad would not see them. I knew he would not let me go anywhere in a car with boys. (He was right, but I didn't know any better.) So they did. The boys went around the block. And once we got into my house, I told Anne Marie that I was afraid of Matt's friend. She said it was okay; she would stick close to me.

I remember wearing one of my older sisters black bathing suits, which was too big for me. It was a two-piece but had a black net on the top that went down to the bottom part making it look like a one-piece bathing suit. I don't recall what Anne Marie put on, but I thought she looked very shapely for fifteen. Luckily for me, my dad was not home.

We met the boys around the corner, and the unsavory boy was in the back seat. Matt was in the driver's seat! I must have turned beet red, because Matt turned to look at Anne Marie and said, "Come on. Sit in the front with me." This left me to sit in the back with this total creep. I was not comfortable sitting in the back seat with a boy. I would imagine that a silly young girl of fifteen might have thought this was so cool, but not me. I had my own instincts, and they were usually right on the money. My instincts were telling me that we were putting ourselves in jeopardy.

I was right!

As we drove up this winding dirt road, covered with bushes everywhere, I again got that gut feeling that this was not a good idea. I tried to lean forward and whisper to Anne Marie that we should insist on going home now. I was feeling really sick. But she didn't turn to me or realize how scared I was at this point. It was too exciting for her now, being with this older boy. Matt was all she cared about at that moment.

After we came to the top of a dirt pathway, we entered a clearing, still in the car. There were many boys there, swimming and hanging around naked, and some were looking straight into the car at us. Anne Marie and Matt jumped out of the front seat right away. And the guys all knew each other, apparently, since they were all shaking hands and whispering as they looked at me in the car. Then Matt's friend got out of the back seat and told me to get out. I said no and refused. Then Anne Marie and Matt disappeared. I had no idea where they had gone and was now terrified of the situation I found myself in.

I was certainly not getting out of that car after seeing naked boys all walking around like it was Grand Central Station. But Matt's friend dragged me out of the car and told me to walk up the hill with him, or he would turn me over to all these naked boys. What choice does a frightened young girl of fifteen have in that moment? What goes through her mind? What fear is she feeling?

I kept telling myself that I was going to try and run the first chance I got. I didn't care where to. I would just run. There were no neighborhoods or houses I could see near the quarries in 1965—just lots of trees, bushes, and rocks that I was unfamiliar with. I was very afraid now, and I began to turn my conscious mind off to the danger I was in. I didn't scream or yell for help. I was sinking into an almost catatonic state of extreme fright.

As Slimy (as I called him) was walking in front of me on this dirt path that seemed to go forever, I could see boys hiding in the bushes just gawking and laughing at me. Oh God I prayed, not now! As Slimy finally sat down on a big rock and told me to sit beside him, he took off his pants and shirt. Now he was naked also! He told me to take off my shorts and my top and to leave my bathing suit on. I begged him no. I started to cry and tremble, but he said to me in a mean voice, "Take them off now, or I'll rip them off you."

I was afraid, but I slowly took my shirt and shorts off, and he said to take my sneakers off too. I asked him if I could just please go. But he said I couldn't leave until I gave him a hand job. And as he said this, he showed me how with his own hands.

Here is where all my guilt had been hiding for so many years. I thought I had provoked this incident because of dressing in a provocative black bathing suit. Slimy said he wasn't going to rape me but just liked my bathing suit and wanted a hand job. In due time, in therapy, I came to realize that I did not have a chance in this situation; it was already planned. I don't think Anne Marie knew what was going to happen to me because she was thinking only of herself and Matt, as I mentioned earlier. Kids do things without realizing the consequences.

I began trembling, and this seemed to turn Slimy on. I just couldn't wait for this to be over so I could go back to the car. I wondered again about Matt and Anne Marie. Where were they? Was she being abused too?

Then it happened. Slimy ejaculated, and I started running. But the boys in the bushes were in the pathway heading down, so I turned around and started running uphill, not knowing where I was going or how I was going to escape this nightmare. The boys were running behind me, laughing and chasing me like a dog.

I was running so hard I didn't even notice the thickets that were scraping my legs or the poison ivy I was running through or the rocks under my feet that were cutting into the soles of my feet. I didn't have a chance. I came to the top of the hill, looked around, and there was nowhere else to run, just lots of bushes and naked boys pursuing me. I just couldn't bear the thought of giving hand jobs again and again to all these boys. That was my fear now—that each one of the boys would force me to give him a hand job. And rightly so. Why else would they be chasing after me?

Now I was at the dead end of the path. I looked down from the edge of the ledge I was standing on—straight down about thirty feet or more was just a round pool of water surrounded by rocks and more naked boys. Even though I knew I couldn't swim, anything was better than turning on all these naked boys, so I *jumped!*

All I could remember after I jumped off that ledge was heading straight down into that water and feeling like knives were going up and down against my body as I went down deeper and deeper into the water. I thought I would never hit bottom.

I could feel my body feeling light and my bathing suit being ripped off me under the water, and that was when I went into shock. It was like all consciousness left me, and I was in a dark place, like a black hole. There was no sound, no talking—just dead silence.

I don't remember coming out of the water that horrible day. And to this day, I still do not know how many of those boys raped me or what I did or what I thought or what I said. I went into complete shock. Every time I try to remember what happened next I come up blank. How did I get home? Why was my vagina in so much pain? Where did I go after this gang rape? I know one thing for sure, I never told anyone. If I did, the boys might have killed me, as they had threatened. I was tempted to go to a hypnotist once I started therapy, but she said doing so might damage my mind further. I may never be able to remember what happened. And if I could, it might cause me irreparable emotional damage.

I had so many questions. But Anne Marie was as distraught as I was and refused to talk to me about it anymore. I don't know how I got home! She did say the boys dropped us off at some field in Dorchester, and I walked home. I can't remember that at all. But if I was in shock, I can understand the blackout.

I just remember that night waking up from under my bed. Everyone was home except my mother. I felt so much pain inside and outside of my body.

The next day was graduation, and I was in a trance the entire time. My mother bought me a beautiful yellow empire dress even though she knew she would not be around for my graduation. My siblings were all working. I had to put calamine lotion on the poison ivy all over me, and fortunately, my mom had Benadryl in the cabinet. I had scrapes all over my legs and arms, and my feet had large cuts all under and over them. I had to wear black nylons with my pretty yellow dress and a sweater to cover my arms. There were bruises on my face and neck and hands that I tried to cover with my sisters' makeup after they left for work. I took the bus to school and felt sick to my stomach. I had no one, no one to run to, just people to run from.

I hated Anne Marie after that, and we stopped being friends. But the next day after graduation, we had to clear out our desks, and she was in the same homeroom as I was. This should have been the happiest day of my youth, but it was far from over.

That next day, I asked her, "What happened? I can't remember."

She said coldly, "Just forget about it!"

Oh my God, I thought. *Is this really happening?*

As Anne Marie and I were leaving the school, we had visitors pull up beside us in front of the school. It was Matt and Slimy and three other ugly-looking boys. They jumped out of the car and stood right in front of us, walking around us as in a circle. They wanted to scare us by telling us what they would do if we told anyone about what had happened at the quarries. First they all took turns telling us how they were going to burn our houses down in the middle of the night while everyone was sleeping if we dared to tell any of our family members about what had taken place.

Then they took turns telling me how they would rape my sisters and break every bone in my brother's body. They were not focusing on Anne Marie so much, I guess because they knew whatever happened between she and Matt was "consensual." I guess now they knew she would never tell.

Matt even told us that his uncle was a judge and would portray us as provocative teasers in court, pointing the blame on us. Then they told me to watch my back; they might follow me and do it all over again. They even bragged about one girl who was gang-raped by these guys who told the police but had to retract her statement because they started a fire at her house in the cellar at 3:00 a.m. fortunately, she and her family had all gotten out. Now I was even more afraid. It seemed like anything they threatened was possible at this point.

Anne Marie never told me what happened to her with Matt that day. She just said she didn't want to talk about it. I was so numb I didn't even care anymore. She had no marks on her and seemed quiet and then distant, while I just walked around repressing all thoughts related to this incident. It was too shocking, confusing, and blank. How could this be? It hurt, but I got over it and never thought about it for twenty-two years.

When it came time to enter ninth grade at a new school, I thought it would make a big difference. I would be at a new school, with new kids, and I would never have to see those boys again.

Wrong. They were there in the eleventh and twelfth grade at the same school. I could not breathe, I could not concentrate, and I was constantly in fear of these gangs. Anne Marie met new friends and didn't include me as her friend anymore. I privately thought it was because of her own guilt for not helping me at the quarries.

I became so unhappy at school that, one day, I asked my mother if I could quit school to go to work and help her pay the bills. She agreed because more money coming into our poor house would be a big help.

I regret every day that I got into the car with Matt and Slimy. And I pray to girls, don't get in a car with boys. I pray that girls and women will follow their own gut feelings and instincts. Your intuition never fails you. So learn to say no as your power tool.

The years went by. I occasionally heard from Anne Marie by way of Christmas cards and birthday cards. She never married. But when I was getting married, I invited her to my wedding. So we started to become friends again. She would visit once in a while. But we never talked about the quarries.

Now twenty-two years later and after a year into therapy, I was working on the rape with my therapist—still drawing a blank as to what happened to me when I came out of the water. I decided to confront Anne Marie, as she was my only witness to what had really gone on after I'd jumped into the water.

I was still in contact with her after all the years, which made it easier for me to approach her. She only lived fifty miles away, so it would be relatively easy to get together. I called her one hot July evening and asked her if I could come down to visit her. I offered to bring some wine and steak so we could have a nice cookout, just the two of us, catching up at her new house near the water. She agreed.

That Sunday in July, I packed up my basket and drove down to see her. My heart was racing, and my mind was full of fear. My body felt ice-cold, and I had the chills. I would always get the chills when I was about to recall and relive a memory that was not so good.

We cooked, ate, and drank our wine. Then we walked along the beach where she lived. We were now adults, me with two babies and her with her own home on the water and a good job. Then I finally came out with the question that had been bothering me for over twenty-three years. I asked her, "Anne Marie, you do remember the quarries incident, don't you?"

And she said, "Yes, very much so."

I then went for the biggest question I could have ever asked anyone in my lifetime. "What happened to me?"

All she could tell me was Matt had held her back from coming to my aid, and all she could hear was my awful screams! I automatically went into my mode of inner silence / inner rage. I wanted to hear the answers, but somehow I felt deaf and couldn't ask any more questions.

Now I know this must sound weird or as if I lack remorse or feelings, but her telling me I screamed gave me some closure to it all. It told me that I did resist and screamed. It reassured me that I was looking for help and was fighting that day! Just knowing someone was there who could tell me I didn't ask for it made a big difference in my life from then on. Knowing a little more about this rape allowed me to deal with it better with my therapist and with other people. It was easy now to talk about it because it had happened so long ago, and no one could hurt me anymore. I couldn't have protected myself back then, and I have now dealt with the reality of that truth and what happened to me through therapy.

I wrote about it just once for an essay I did in college. This was when I went back to school at age thirty-six. But that was the last time I could write about it until now. And I didn't have a clue why. I wrote it without any feelings, just as an assignment.

Every time I tried to write about the quarries, I would choke up or I would say, "No. I can't do this." Even though I knew sharing my story might help someone out there who had experienced something similar, I had not been able to write about the trauma till I was in therapy and going into college.

When I decided to write this story, it was very hard. I wanted to reach out to other victims. But how could I, when I didn't really know what happened? I've learned, though, through determination and therapy, that it doesn't matter what happened that caused me to "black out." The only thing that matters is I survived to tell about it.

The moral to my story: Don't get in a car with strangers. Listen to your gut feelings. And stand firm!

CHAPTER 5

The Second Rape: Lessons Learned

After the rape at the Quincy quarries, I became paranoid about everything. I felt as if someone was watching me from a bush across the street or behind a car, from behind a doorway, or from down any alleyway I passed. Or I just thought someone was walking behind me. I didn't want to be friends with anyone. I had learned from the gang rape and my best friend's desertion of me never to trust anyone. I didn't want to go back to that school. And fortunately for me, we were moving again.

We were now moving from Hyde Park to Jamaica Plain. And to be honest, I was glad we were moving out of my hometown—the town I was born in and thought I'd never leave. I felt relieved that I wouldn't have to see those boys from the quarries ever again. I was moving to a new town, where no one knew me or had ever heard of me—or so I thought. But something really bad was about to happen to me again while I was living at this new house in this new town I had been happy to get to.

This new apartment building was very different from the other houses I'd lived in. It was a brick building with three floors. We lived on the first floor, but this building connected to another building that was exactly the same. It was called a brownstone, and the two buildings were connected with no alley in between. We lived on the first floor, with windows in the front and the back but none on the sides. There was a badly worn-out porch in the back, which I could never go on. It was dark, and planks of wood were missing from the floor. That made me sad, as I'd always loved my porches. I recall that our three-bedroom apartment in that brownstone was very dark inside.

I was starting to feel older now that I was fifteen, almost sixteen. I was more aware of myself now, whereas before I had just been numb. Back in September 1965, you could get your driver's permit and your working papers and actually get a job at that age, and that was my plan. I quit school in Hyde Park after being enrolled for only two weeks. I'd convinced my mother that, if I quit, I could work and help pay the bills. I withheld from her my real reason for wanting to leave school—the prospect of seeing those boys from the quarry on a regular basis. And she readily agreed.

Once we moved into the new apartment, I also managed to talk my brother into taking me for driving lessons. He did. I was almost sixteen and would be that November. I don't know why I wanted to drive so badly. Maybe I was looking for a distraction or a faster way of running away from things. I had no car or any idea of how I could get one. I had only just started working and didn't have nearly enough money. But I knew and felt I'd get a car soon enough.

During the transition from Hyde Park to Jamaica Plain, my mother found a job at a nearby hospital. It was so close to our new place that she could walk to work. My dad, once more, was in jail for cashing bad checks. She got a job in the housekeeping department. She was only fifty-three at this time in her life. I was maturing and started to realize how much my mother had gone through; she'd endured so much pain and adversity during her marriage.

After getting my working papers, I joined her at this hospital and applied for a job in the kitchen, working in the dietary kitchen under the supervision of four adults. My job would be to prepare food trays for the patients and deliver the trays to their rooms. I would deliver trays to the patients on three floors in the main building. I would also go through a tunnel to the adjacent building and deliver trays to that floor. The work—delivering the trays and then picking them up and taking them back to the kitchen for cleanup—kept me very busy.

I got along with everyone, loved my job, and enthusiastically performed my work each day. This was my first job and the first time I did not have to go to school. I felt exhilarated for the first time in my life because of these two changes.

Our work at the hospital was less than a fifteen-minute walk from our apartment, which made working there quite convenient and pleasurable. At first I was hired as part-time help due to my age. But when I turned sixteen, I moved up to working full-time. This workplace was a big factor in my feeling much better about myself. This was a happy place for me. Everyone was very friendly and helpful.

I felt good there. I used to write poems and read them to anyone who wanted to listen. I always got excited about all the positive feedback I received, so I just kept writing more poems all the time.

One day I had to work a shift from 7:00 a.m. to 7:00 p.m. and was walking home. It was a short walk, as I noted earlier. As I was approaching the square that I had to walk through to get to my street, I noticed a bunch of boys hanging out in front of the general store. Naturally I panicked. It had only been six months since I had been gang-raped. As I was walking past the boys (who didn't look or act like tough boys), I heard one of the boys call out my name.

I thought to myself, *Oh my God, no. Don't let this be anyone from Hyde Park.* But to my surprise, it was a boy named Freddy who I'd gone to school in the seventh grade.

Freddy was a funny kid at school, always playing pranks on kids. For instance, one time while I was in the seventh grade and fourteen years old, I had to go to the girls' room. Back in those days, there would be a school monitor outside the restroom doors. You were required to write your name and the time you arrived at the girls' room into a notebook that the monitor had, and Freddy was the monitor. I signed in, and he cracked a joke. I just ignored him.

After I came out of the girls' room, I had to sign out, again writing down the time. Freddy was still talking when I signed out, and as I started walking back to my home room, he yelled out, "Hey, you. There's some toilet paper still stuck to your skirt."

I must have turned ten shades of red and turned around embarrassed as hell, and there was no toilet paper on my skirt. I just gave him such a look he said he never forgot me.

Sometime after that incident, one of my friends from the projects was having a party, and I was there. So was Freddy. He tried to talk to me, but I was still mad at him. I should have talked to him because he was a nice kid, and he was good-looking. My family had to move out of the projects after that, and I never saw him again until this night on my way home from work.

To my surprise, I stopped and started talking to him. He was now a little older, as was I, and we had a nice talk. Then he asked me if he could walk me home.

I said, "Sure."

We became friends. He was still in school and lived five streets over from my new apartment. He had no car, and neither did I. So we used to hang out at the schoolyard at the bottom of my street.

I had always gravitated toward boys as friends. Now I had a new friend in my new neighborhood. We never got intimate, although he tried to kiss me once at the beginning of our friendship. I said no. I was very up front with him and told him about the quarries rape. It was the first time I'd ever told anyone. And from then on, he respected my feelings. He showed me empathy and was becoming someone, way back then, who showed me kindness. And he swore he'd never tell anyone about what had happened to me.

Unfortunately, just as I was beginning to learn how to trust again, another trauma lay ahead of me. Another travesty was lying in wait, ready to fill up my already badly beaten self-worth and to be added to my bag of inner silence / inner rage.

I met a lot of new friends during this time. All of them were from my workplace. I made friends from the kitchen, the cafeteria, the coffee shop, and the gift shop. I even befriended the dispatch lady. And of course, I had friendships with many of the staff from the housekeeping department where my mother worked.

I was always open, friendly, and happy. I felt vastly different that I had just six months ago. I used to love to tell jokes. Making others laugh was my way of cultivating as many new friends as possible. I thought that would lessen the chances of anyone disliking me and trying to hurt me.

That night when I'd met back up with Freddy, I had noticed there was an older guy hanging around the front of the general store, leaning on a white Cadillac and talking to the boys. He looked out of place with these younger boys, and when I turned around to check on Freddy's friends, I asked Freddy, "Who's that older guy?"

Freddy just laughed and said, "Oh, that's Big Jim."

I don't know why, but he gave me the creeps. Nonetheless, I left it at that and went home.

It was sometime later—a few months after I'd moved to Jamaica Plain, gotten a job, and started a friendship with Freddy—when a car pulled up next to me at the corner of my street. I had just gotten off work. Again, I was doing a 7:00 a.m. to 7:00 p.m. shift, and I was very tired and almost home. It was Big Jim in his white Cadillac who was approaching me.

Just when I was starting to feel a little confident he caught me off guard, and I started to feel uncomfortable. He said from his car window, "I need to talk to you about Freddy."

"Why?" I replied. "What's wrong with him?"

"Please just get in the car for a minute," said Big Jim. "I can't talk about it out there."

Why didn't I go with my gut instinct and not get into the car? I never could understand that until I got older and underwent therapy, which, along with my self-help books, provided the tools that finally woke me up. I had no self-worth, no self-esteem, and no power. Why is it that I knew and felt something creepy about this guy but still got into his car? I had done the same thing the day of the quarries rape. I guess I was more concerned or worried about Freddy than I was about myself.

How could I let my guard down? I could have said, "No. Get out of your car and we can talk." Why, after getting in the car with that creep Slimy from the quarries rape, would I ever get into a stranger's car again? It had only been six months since I'd gotten into the wrong car, so I can't understand why I got into Big Jim's car. What did I want to hear that couldn't just as well have been heard if he'd talked to me on the sidewalk? What did I not learn from the gang rape? How could I be so naive?

It happened so quickly, and I knew I was in danger right away. The minute I got into the car, he locked the car doors with his automatic lock.

He started driving down my street, and I asked him, "What do you want to talk about concerning Freddy?"

He just laughed and said, "I have nothing to say about Freddy. It's you I want."

I was instantly on the verge of panic or wetting my pants. A shiver ran up and down my spine. I could tell he was going to do something to me against my will. He said, "We're just going to go for a little ride."

I kept silent, trying to figure a way out of this trap. I couldn't think of any way out, as he had control of the door locks from the driver's side.

He pulled up to a drive-in movie theater, a popular site back in my day. He paid for the tickets and parked way in the back, where no other cars were. I thought for sure I had gotten the message at the quarries never to trust a boy or a man, but I was wrong. Big Jim never intended to talk to me about Freddy. He only wanted to force himself on me so he could go brag about it to all the guys, including Freddy. Once he parked the car and slid over to me (now remember, this is back in 1965; most cars did not have a middle console; the front seat was one long seat you could seat three people in) I started to scream. He put his hand over my mouth and pulled my hair back so forcefully I thought he was going to break my neck. I can vividly remember every moment of this encounter like it was yesterday.

At this point, he slid further over to me and said, "Open the glove compartment."

I did what he told me, trembling and not daring to speak. I was shaking just like I always do when something is wrong, but I never said a word the entire time. There in the glove compartment was a gun. And as he reached in for it, I felt like I was going to throw up or be killed. I became terribly frightened and horrified, but he was calm. He knew he had all the power. He put the gun to my head and mouth and told me he was going to do whatever he wanted with me and that I couldn't do or say a thing about it, unless of course I wanted to be shot and left there. It wouldn't be the first time, he said. It was extremely frightening, and I knew I just wanted to live and go home and hide under my bed if this ordeal ever ended!

He made me get undressed completely, which made me feel embarrassed. I remember how cold I was and having this animal inside me didn't make me any warmer. He made sure he kept the glove compartment opened so I could see the gun that he'd pressed against my head and mouth. After that initial threat, he'd placed the gun back into the open glove compartment for me to see and be aware of its presence. I thought several times of reaching for it, but I was too afraid. He was much bigger than I was, besides being about twenty years older than me and stronger.

I felt like I was still a child, and he was the adult. My inner silence / inner rage was boiling inside of me again. I had no strength or power to fight off this animal. I asked myself, *Why did he pick me?*

Why didn't I try to run? He had the automatic lock on, and when I screamed, he put his hand across my mouth. He intimidated me until I just shut down and never said another word to him. I felt I had to keep silent to be safe. I could have begged like I did at the quarries rape, but I knew that would get me nowhere. I knew the answer was that rapists don't care, so I just kept silent and numb.

For what felt like several hours, he abused me. The torture of his heavy body on mine, the pulling of my hair, the biting of my breasts, the turning me front to back like a rag doll, the heavy breathing, the filthy words—I can recall every minute of me. I was a cunt, a whore, a dirty girl. Fuck him. Fuck you. He would wring my neck until I almost choked to death. It was like he was in a marathon, abusing me and amusing himself. To this day, I can describe everything that happened in that car so clearly. I remembering telling myself, *Stay calm. It's your body that's being violated, not your mind.* So I took my mind off the rape and went into a black hole!

He finished and was covered with sweat. Then smiling at me, he patted my hair. He finally started getting dressed and told me to get dressed. I never said a word to him. I hadn't spoken once since I sensed I knew what he was going to do with me.

I had mastered this intense sense of intuition and was able to remove my mind from my body during the repulsive rape. That's how I got through it. I'd trained my mind to do this well. I could actually see myself leaving the assault, floating above myself calmly, and silently going into my own black abyss until it was over, not thinking at all. It was just one more nightmare and trauma that I had to endure. Only this time, I remembered everything.

He dropped me off at the corner of my street, which was the corner of the square. I began praying he wouldn't tell anyone. Then he said through his rotten smile, "I'll be seeing you again!"

Not if I could help it.

He also said he would kill me if I did anything stupid like calling the police or telling my parents. And the memory of those boys at the quarries rape saying similar things surfaced in my mind. I had learned to be intimidated and to keep silent. Inner silence / inner rage was present during this entire rape.

My mom was in the kitchen when I got home, and I asked her if I could just go to bed. I told her I was beat after work, and she said, "Okay, but do the dishes in the morning."

I just went into the room that I shared with my one of my sisters. She was out in the living room watching TV. I put on my pajamas, grabbed a pillow and a blanket off the bed, and crawled under the bed to cry myself to sleep. My entire body was hurting. My mother never suspected anything was wrong with me.

I cried, but then something inside me kept saying, *Take a hot bath*. So I left my room and went straight for the tub. I relaxed in that hot water tub until I felt that every part of me was clean and free from that animal rapist's intrusion into my body.

My body was free of him, but my mind wasn't. I was wondering what had happened to me. Big Jim had put a rubber thing on his penis (it was the first time I'd ever seen one), and it had hurt terribly when he'd plunged into my body.

I never saw or heard of Big Jim again after the rape, thank God! Freddy told me he went to jail. *Good*, I thought to myself. And I never told Freddy about what Big Jim had done to me. I just wanted it silenced and forgotten.

What is the lesson I learned from this incident? It wasn't so much about not getting in the car with a stranger as it was about building up your self-esteem and courage. The lesson I learned is that you can protect yourself emotionally all you want by remaining silent and burying your bad memories. Protecting your physical welfare until you develop healthy self-esteem and courage to fight back and say no is another story. I know that, if I cared enough about myself, I never would have gotten in the car or even talked to that creep guy. The lesson was that it's imperative to go with your first gut feeling; that's an instinct that should not be ignored.

If something or someone doesn't feel right, then you should know what to do automatically. This doesn't just apply to rape. It could be knowing where to draw the line if someone is being mean to you. It could be that, if you sense that other girls are jealous of you, you need to avoid them, since they could cause you trouble. What I'm trying to say is be careful who you choose as a friend and find someone you can trust. Stay around positive people. You have the power to attract positive people to you. Build your self-esteem by participating in sports or even karate.

I learned the hard way how to be self-reliant, which was an important lesson. But I learned a "bad lesson" from the attacks that I endured too—I learned that I needed to be in control all the time, and that represented fear. Through therapy, I've learned a lot about myself in relation to all the experiences and traumas I've been through. That emotion of vigilant fear, integrated into the fabric of my being, was the hardest obstacle to overcome on the road to becoming an emotionally healthy person. It took years for me to recognize and deal with it in a healthy manner.

After the night of my second rape, I became more aware of what to wear. Controlling my appearance through clothing choices was a survival tactic I used. And so I began to dress very conservatively at age sixteen. I didn't want to look like those half-naked girls in *Teen* magazine. I believed that dressing that way only drew unwanted attention from boys. So I avoided tight or revealing clothes. I missed out completely on being a silly, giggly teenage girl. I was too old before my time because of these rape incidents.

I worked as many hours as I could and bought myself my own car. I learned how to judge the bad kids from the good kids and befriended the good kids, because I knew they wouldn't hurt me. Good work ethics nourished my goal of inner peace, and working to better myself became the foremost activity in my life back then. Now, though, I have fun with my inner peace because I don't have to work as hard at it anymore.

We stayed at this apartment in Jamaica Plain for about nine months until my father came home from jail and announced that we were moving again. This would be the eighth house for me at age sixteen, going on 17. I wish I had read a book like this when I was sixteen.

I believe I had to go through all these horrible experiences in order to write this book and help others who are burying their traumas and to have them believe in me. I want to try and help as many people as I can with what ability I have. I have the experience, but I'm not a teacher. I am an emotional, driven woman who wants to reach out to as many people who are out there hurting as possible. I believe, once they read my story, they can find a way to acknowledge their emotional wounds and find the courage to get help.

So, my dear reader, I hope I have enlightened you a little bit through sharing my personal experiences. And I hope that you too can start a fresh journey—a journey that will be meaningful and playful. After all, within you is an inner child waiting to come out and play.

So play!

CHAPTER 6

Death and Guilt

I thought that moving to house number eight would be great. This new apartment was a duplex house with plenty of sunshine and windows. Not to mention, I got my own room for the first time in my seventeen years. We were still in Jamaica Plain and only a train ride away from my job at the hospital. My mom and dad were getting along better in this new house too. But with the sun comes the rain.

This chapter will be another really difficult one for me to write. Actually they were all very hard to write. I endured so many hard times. But they were lessons, as I call them now when I write. What did I learn from my experiences? Sorry, my dear reader, but I don't think I learned my lessons well until I sought help. I will try to be as accurate as possible in recording the events that next shaped my life. One thing I did not lose up to age eighteen was my memory.

My feelings, on the other hand, well, let's say they were sleeping silently somewhere inside of my inner silence / inner rage. I have since learned many emotions—adversity, grief, loneliness, sadness, pain, hurt, and betrayal just to mention a few—all within two years.

While I was still working at the hospital in the kitchen, I met this boy, John, who worked in the kitchen as well. He liked me a lot. Even though I was sixteen, almost seventeen, I still did not date. It's not that I thought all boys and men were jerks due to the rapes. I just didn't trust anyone except my friend Freddy. And all I wanted was friends, not boyfriends. All the girls at the hospital who I hung out with were dating boys. But I just liked being on my own—with no boyfriends—even though I didn't even realize what having a boyfriend meant.

Yet one day John from the kitchen department asked me out to the movies, the drive-in. I had been working there for months now, and I thought I knew everyone. I don't know why I said yes, because I really didn't like this boy all that well. I should have said, "No, thank you."

He was always pulling pranks on all of us who worked in the kitchen department, and he was constantly following me around. He had his own car, and I had my own car. I'd bought mine myself with the help of my brothers. It was a 1961 Chevy Impala convertible with an eight-track tape in it that was constantly playing Herb Albert and the Tijuana Brass band—not your average teenage music for the '60s, but I was way beyond my time. I worked sixty hours a week in order to buy that car for five hundred dollars back in 1966.

I became self-reliant at an early age, and I vowed no one would ever hurt me again. I would never put myself in harm's way ever again as I had done in the past.

I was very intuitive now, always watching for the other shoe to drop as the saying goes. And I was very independent. Self-sufficient, I trusted no one but kept my enemies very close to me so I would know what they were up to.

But John just seemed harmless and funny. Everyone in the kitchen liked him, so I did go to the drive-in. And we had a good time. He constantly made you laugh. He loved to joke and to play tricks on people. For example, he said to me at the drive-in, "I'll be right back. Wait here in the car."

Well, he was taking so long I got out of the car and went looking for him. I searched the recession stand and the boys' room, but he was nowhere—like he'd disappeared!

I got back to the car. There he was in the driver's seat, chirping up into laughter and saying, "What took you so long?"

I could have killed him.

During the summer, we would have every other weekend off. So we would go family visiting. My family liked him a lot, as he was always laughing or telling stories and jokes. Along with being so amusing, he was very clean-cut—unlike the "hippies" who were so abundant back in 1967. John would take me to visit his mother and grandmother, who he lived with. They both liked me and said I was a blessing to John. I use to sit for hours doing a jigsaw puzzle with his grandmother, which was very pleasant.

But then I started wondering if something wasn't normal with John. One of his last pranks while we were hanging out was odd. I couldn't handle it. I drove down to his house one Sunday afternoon with a new puzzle for his grandmother and flowers for his mom. As I approached the house, John was in the driveway washing his car. When I got out of my car, he started spraying water from the hose all over me. I was screaming, "Stop it! Stop it!" But he kept laughing till his mother came out of the house yelling at him, and then he stopped. I was in shock!

His mother brought out some towels and was drying my hair and back as I stood there shivering. Strangely, she did not say anything to him. John came over to me, looking all innocent and said to me, "I just wanted to cool you off. It's a hot day."

That was when I definitively knew he was not all there.

Luckily for me, I had my own car. I told him off and drove away. Back in my day, there were no cell phones. But by the time I got home some forty-five minutes later, my mother said John has been constantly calling the house. I never said anything to my family about the incident because I knew they liked him quite a lot. I did, however, say I didn't want to be his girlfriend. He was just a friend; that was all. And yes, once more, this was one more traumatizing event to add to my badly beaten inner silence / inner rage.

When I saw John that Monday at work, he apologized like crazy. But I said to him calmly, "I just want us to be friends and no more dating."

I could tell he was devastated. But what did I know about his obsession with me? I'd never had been with a boy till him, and we were not intimate at all. I was like ice when it came to hugging or even kissing. Well, he kept trying to call me. Or he would show up at my house unexpectedly. So I had no choice but to write him what we called a "Dear John letter." In the letter, I told him it wasn't his fault, but I didn't want anything to do with him anymore and asking to stop calling my house!

He was devastated, distraught, and sad at work. One Sunday night, all the girls from work, myself included, were going to the local hangout, the Hop. John was walking behind us and called out, "Kathy."

I turned to look at him, not knowing how brokenhearted he really was. I said calmly and quietly, "What?"

"Turn your car radio on at 9:00 p.m.," he told me. (That was when the local station played the oldies on Sunday nights.)

I didn't ask why. I just said, "Sure."

All us girls were having a soda and went to sit in my car in a parking lot. I turned on the radio and tuned into the oldies hour exactly at 9:00 p.m. The first song played was "Cathy's Clown," which was being dedicated to Kathy from John. I felt terrible, yet the girls were all laughing.

The next morning was a Monday, and when I woke up, I had this terrible feeling something was wrong. I didn't know why. But suddenly, my older brother, who drove a taxi and who liked John, came rushing through the front door. I jumped up and ran to the top of the staircase. Looking down at my brother, I said the first thing that came to my mind. "It's John, isn't it?"

"Yes," he said. "How did you know?"

"Know what?" I asked. "Something awful has happened to him, right?"

My brother nodded and said "Yes, he was in a head-on collision with another car last night. Everyone involved is dead!"

I sat at the top of the stairs, ready to throw up and shaking and finally wailing my head off just thinking about the "Dear John" letter I had written him just two weeks ago. I was in total shock when my brother told me that John was driving on the wrong side of the road at a fast rate of speed and had caused the collision. More wailing and crying ensued. Guilt was setting in to my already filled bag of traumas.

My brother was a taxi driver and had heard the news immediately on his two-way radio. He said "Sorry, sis, but I've got to get back to work."

This was around 6:00 a.m.

I'd met John's family several times, and they really liked me. So when I went to the wake and the family ignored me, I couldn't understand what was going on. I tugged on his brother's arm and asked how he was doing. With what came next, I literally almost fell to the floor.

"When the fire department extracted John from the wreck," he told me, "they found your letter clenched in his fist."

I left the funeral parlor shaking and crying. I felt out of control and was crying out loudly and saying, "This was all my fault."

My sister got out of her car and came racing toward me. Shaking me, she said, "Stop it! Stop it right now!"

I finally sunk into my familiar black hole and kept silent—already turning inward into my now familiar inner silence / inner rage. I felt so guilty and wished I had never written that letter! I had never thought he would do something like this.

I never told anyone about that letter I gave to John. It breaks my heart even today when I look back and think of him.

The next two months working in the kitchen department were very hard for me. But I just kept asking my manager for more hours, as many as I could get. I wanted to keep myself busy so I could continue burying my emotions—once more folding them into my growing inner silence / inner rage. I would write every night, composing poems on forgiveness, loneliness, and grief.

The girls from the kitchen department kept hounding me to come out with them to the Hop. So after two months of grieving, I finally joined them. I started to relax and laugh again. I was still only seventeen years old and was still very naive.

Then one night, a boy came over to us girls in my car. He knew the other girls and said to me, "Nice car," (referring to my '61 Chevy convertible).

I was smitten by him but held back my pounding heart.

The girls hushed him away and then told me, "He likes you."

"Who is he?" I asked.

They said his name was Walter and that he lived three streets over from me. He'd been asking, "Who's the new girl? And does she have a boyfriend?" (They didn't tell me he was a girl watcher.)

Then it happened. The next weekend, all we girls went to the Hop to hang out. I went inside the Hop to get a cup of hot tea, and who was following me? It was that boy, Walter. He introduced himself, and he said would love to buy me that cup of tea.

Inside of me, I felt butterflies that I'd never felt before. I was trying to be calm and said, "Okay."

We sat at the counter talking and found we had a lot in common. Then, bingo, he asked me for a formal date at a nice steak house—very impressive to the young naive girl that I was. I couldn't believe I said, "Okay!"

This was Saturday, and he said, "How about tomorrow? Say around 1:00 p.m.?" I was still too stunned to answer when he added, "And don't worry. I know where you live."

CHAPTER 7

The Abortion

Walter and I fell in love right away. We still both worked and saw each other all the time, including every weekend. It was as if we could not get enough of each other. We were drawn to each other in a heated hunger and could not wait to see each other. We would sit in the car and kiss, steaming up all the windows.

Walter was an only child and loved my large family, who adored him. His parents loved me too. Everything seemed so perfect. To make a long story short, I finally found out what a boyfriend was and fell head over heels for my first.

Just about a month into dating and fighting off the wall I had built around my feelings, I finally gave in to his sexual advances. And for the first time in my young life, sex was consensual. All my pain about sex melted away, and I began to trust. Unfortunately, that was short-lived.

Walter and I had been seeing each other for six months when I got pregnant at seventeen. I was about two months pregnant, the doctor said. I was so happy and could not wait to tell Walter. I thought of how happy we would be.

But Walter said no! He said, "This will wreck our own growing years."

"I want to have this baby," I insisted.

But he was adamant. "Do you realize I could go to jail for this because you are still considered a minor?" he asked. He was five years older than me.

I was still very naive and gullible and listened to every word he said. He talked me out of having the baby. I had no self-worth or self-esteem that would enable me to stick up for myself, so I let him take over. He knew of a place in New York that would perform abortions (it was not legal in my state).

We took the bus to New York, and he paid for the abortion fee. The place was a dirty, old brick building with filthy windows that you could not look out of. The elevator trains flying by the building made it rattle. I wanted to run. But to where? Walter left me there the minute he paid the guy and said he would be back that night. I was in such a state of panic and shock that I let him talk me into this mess.

The reality, had I not let him take control, was that I would have been a single parent. And thinking back now, I see that would not have been so bad.

I regretted the abortion and began to hate him. Meanwhile, he could not stress enough how it was not the time for us to be married, as we were too young. I had no one to call to come and get me in New York, I didn't even know what city I was in. Plus this was the '60s, when cell phones or beepers did not yet exist.

My parents had no money, and my father probably would have slapped me around for sure had I decided to stay pregnant. All I could think about was the negative things that would result from having this baby. No one was there to tell me it was going to be okay—to say, "Have your baby."

The thought of terminating the pregnancy killed me inside, and my head hurt badly. I was terribly afraid and did not know where to run.

The procedure was horrific. The providers didn't knock us girls out. They just did this salt injection and sent us back to the mats covering the floor in this giant room that looked like a warehouse till we felt cramps. Then we were taken back to the operating room, where a suction-like apparatus was attached to our privates. Next, we were pushed off the table as the provider said, "Next," like we were cattle ready for the slaughterhouse. (Reliving this trauma as I write still makes my heart race.) Finally, our pained bodies were brought back into the large warehouse room, where dirty, stained mats covered the floors, no clean sheets to be found. I looked around at all the other girls lying down on these dirty mats. All of us, myself included, were crying.

The whole process was very degrading and damaging to my very core. I kept screaming in this room, "It's not all out. The baby is still moving inside me."

So the doctor, in order to shut me up, took me back to the operating room and started the suction machine again. All I could see was blood. Trauma was setting in, and I went into my black abyss—totally numb and in shock.

The termination of my pregnancy was my one and only regret. And I had to live with that regret, as whether or not to have the baby was my choice to make. But I didn't choose; instead, I listened to Walter. Remorse and guilt would creep up into my mind for years as I watched others having babies and loving them, caressing and cuddling them. I was so sad I became hard after this. I never told anyone except one sister about the abortion and begged her not to tell anyone, and she never did.

Walter showed up around 8:00 p.m. that night, and we silently sat on the bus ride home, not speaking a word to each other at all. I was filled up with regret. How had this happened? How had I let my guard down? Why had I trusted him? Could I not see through him or myself that he was the wrong guy?

What at seventeen years old did I feel from losing my baby? It was too painful to let my emotions out. The anger was there, but the silence prevailed.

After Walter got me home, he did not call me for four days.

I told my mother I had a bad cold, and she made me chicken soup and would check on me sleeping every day for the next four days. All I could do was lay there in my bed, crying and remembering the entire ordeal.

Then Walter finally showed up at my parents' house. He came up to my room. Both my parents were working. He said he'd had more bad news, and he'd gone on a bender with the guys.

I said coldly, "What could be so bad that it caused you to abandon me and make me have an abortion?"

Then he said, "I have been activated to the war for a year."

I remember asking God, "Why?" But no answer came, and he was leaving the following week. It was 1967. I would be eighteen years old in one month.

We managed to be civil and to lean on each other that week. Trying to forgive him and myself was very hard. But I really did love him, and I promised I would write every day, which I did.

I worked harder and was promoted from the dead-end kitchen job to an office job through the administration department. I also met some new girls to want me to join their bowling league.

"Sure," I said. "Why not?

I really had no life I felt.

I also went back to school at eighteen years old for a two-year program so I could get my diploma.

I never looked for or asked for help back then. I should have. But being conditioned by how I'd handled all my other traumas, I found that silence was the only thing I knew how to do. Regret was a new emotion I now felt. If only I had learned to reach out along my journey, without such guilt and shame, I would have been a happier girl, with or without Walter.

I really did have a support group at home. And I do not fully understand why I didn't let my family members inside my brain—why I didn't let them help me.

Because of my past, I felt guilty, disgraced, and unloved. I was conditioned to shut up and be silent. I had created the now familiar inner silence / inner rage, as it was easier than dealing with the hurt I had to endure.

I kept silent about this one incident for many years. But the rage lived on. And every month in May, I would torture myself once more thinking about the baby I would have delivered back when I thought I knew what love was all about and what it was like to have a real boyfriend.

CHAPTER 8

The Third Rape

While Walter was away overseas in the war, I worked plenty of hours and went back to school. I also joined a bowling league with some new friends. Upstairs from the bowling alley was a small restaurant that served pizza and had a jukebox. We girls would play records and dance to them. On the adjacent side, there was a bar. It allowed men only, and no one under twenty-one could go in there.

One night, this husky, burly-looking guy about twenty years my senior who was a regular and who hung out with the guys on the other side came over to us girls. But he directed his request to me, asking me if I could drive him into Boston. This was after bowling, and we girls were eating our pizza and drinking our coke and playing the jukebox. For some reason, this older guy didn't concern me, and I asked him, "Why not take a taxi?"

His reason was he needed someone new to drive him to a place where I would wait in my car for an hour while he did some business. Then I would drive him home locally, where he lived with his wife and children nearby. It seemed innocent enough to me.

The girls were all giggling. And he said, "Ask anyone here. I'm a good guy. Plus, I'll pay you a hundred dollars for your time and the ride."

Back in my day, that was like a million dollars, so I said, "Okay," without ever thinking of the danger or consequences.

I'd never seen a one hundred-dollar bill in 1968, and I was still naive and innocent. Even though my thoughts went to what I'd learned from my past—never get into the car with a stranger—I figured this was reversed. I had the car. I had the control. I was not thinking straight. Here I was about ready, for the third time, to get into a bad situation with a stranger, no matter whose car.

By 9:30 p.m. that night, the bowling crew was leaving, so I drove him into Boston. He insisted on sitting in the back seat, but I never questioned him as to why.

I drove him into Boston about five times within two months without any incidents. So I felt comfortable with him and felt he was no threat. One time, he brought along two hookers from the bowling alley bar. As I drove them into Boston, they were drinking and kissing him. I could hear all the advances that were going on in the back seat of my car. I didn't fear him, as I thought I was quite modest and plain. He wouldn't touch me, right?

This one night, I waited to till 1:00 a.m., and he finally came back to my car and sat in the back seat as usual. He directed me to drive him home, which was local. I knew where the townhouses were. Lots of complexes and lots of trees surrounded this place, so when I drove him home to his place, it was always dark and no one was around.

He got out of the car and thanked me, but as I started to drive away, he called me back and said he couldn't find his keys. I parked the car, got out of the driver's side, and was bending over looking for his keys in the back seat floor behind the driver's side when I felt him right behind me, ripping my pants down. "Shut the fuck up, or I'll strangle you right here, and no one will know," he said.

Again panic flowed through me. My brain scrambled to figure out, *How can I get out of this?* He was holding my head very hard against the top of the car door roof. It was so intense I thought for sure I was dying or I was going to die. I couldn't move. Then the rush of his filthy mouth telling me to shut up reminded me clearly of the last two rapes.

Why me? I was just (or so I thought I was) kind and helpful. I was an innocent, young, clean-cut girl. I didn't attract this, no. But I sure did put myself in danger by accepting his request for a ride the first time. I should have been more aware of strangers. I should have asked myself, what is the possible danger of allowing this stranger into my personal space? Then he never would have gotten into my car!

He first went from behind me and pushed both of my arms up behind my back, which was extremely painful and made any move I made intolerable. It was 3:00 a.m. and very dark in his parking lot. I believed him when he said, "Shut the fuck up or I'll kill you right here. I can snap your neck, and you will die."

Then he put his huge penis into my vagina from behind me with such a thrust I thought I was seeing stars. He pulled out of my vagina and then proceeded to sodomize me (entering his penis into my rectum). A rush of terrible pain plunged into my body. I almost fainted. I'd never had rectal sex before. And believe me, to this day I never have after that fateful night.

He was quick, but the assault seemed to last forever to me. Those were the longest minutes I'd ever had to endure. This was my third rape, and I kept asking myself, why? What did I ever do to attract these horrible animals into my life? I'd always thought I was a good girl. I never flirted, never did drugs, and never hung out with groups. I didn't expose my body by wearing tight clothes. I didn't even wear makeup back then. I was friendly but still thought I was cautious and in control of myself and my life.

So the lesson I hadn't gotten yet was, no matter whose car you're in, don't let strangers in. All I could think about was, how will this affect me and Walter? Should I tell him? He was coming home in three months.

The strangest part of this rape was that I felt guilty for driving this strange man around in exchange for one hundred dollars. I hadn't thought anything could go wrong. I still carried around with me my low self-esteem and didn't think anyone would want me for lust. Why not the other girls? They certainly were prettier than me I thought. I was attracting bad things by keeping silent. I never realized I had any rights. I had only fear back then, and fear was my poison!

I yelled at this man and drove home. My rectum was bleeding, and I felt so much pain. The next morning I was at school and had to use the ladies room. All this white stuff gushed out of my rectum. I felt afraid. I thought, *How can I avoid anything bad anymore?* I was losing hope of having a happy life.

I immediately stopped the bowling league and stopped seeing my new friends from up there at the bowling alley.

I started feeling depressed. On top of that, the guilt I felt was overwhelming. How hard I was on myself was a nightmare. I was endlessly putting myself down; self-loathing sunk in.

It was like my life ended. I couldn't call the police on this guy, as while driving him into Boston, I'd heard he was a bookie and a real bad guy. Yet I had never seen it for what it was until that night. I didn't even know his name. (He died in prison not long after this incident).

All the scary things that could happen came rushing in. I was already so conditioned to fear of what the rapists could do that I had no hope or trust.

I worked all week and slept in every weekend till Walter came home. I had developed colitis (bleeding rectally) from this last rape. That threw me over the edge physically, attacking my nervous system and gastric intestines. I was on medication and was making monthly visits to the doctors to try and control this disease. But sadly to say, I unconsciously living in fear, and my stomach took the brunt of it.

I just wanted to be alone in my world of inner silence/inner rage. Shutting down was my only way of coping with life as it was.

CHAPTER 9

Betrayal and Venereal Disease

While Walter was away at war, I wrote to him every day. He also asked me if I could write letters to some of the soldiers who had no one, and I said sure. Then a friend of mine from the hospital was also activated, so I wrote to him a lot. Walter wrote me 326 letters while he was away.

Walter was a happy, loving guy till the abortion. But throughout the lonely year apart during the war and through his letters and mine, our connection grew, and we were back in love wholeheartedly.

When Walter finally came home from the war, his entire demeanor had changed, although he said he wanted to marry me. Before he left, he had been a clean-cut, well-shaven conservative; a nonsmoker; and a happy guy. But no, I was not getting my Walter back. The war had changed him into someone I didn't know anymore. He wore his scars on his sleeve, the pain and suffering he must have gone through and seen evident. I didn't see what he had seen, though, and I didn't get it. More importantly, Walter was now big into weed and hanging out with a new set of guy's two towns over.

I was trying to get my life back, as the third rape had now taken me on an emotional, depressing ride. And I didn't like it or myself. I was trying to fix it all, but I couldn't fix Walter. I couldn't even fix me.

I got violently ill one day and drove myself to the emergency room at the local hospital, not the hospital I worked at. I got a diagnosis; I had contracted gonorrhea, a venereal disease that you only could get from having sex. Walter was the only person I'd had sex with once he came home from the war, and that was six months earlier. This sort of disease could sit in a woman's body for up to six months before showing pain and distress.

It was bad, and I had to be admitted into the hospital. I called my sister and told her where I was as an inpatient and that I'd be there for three days. I begged her again, "Please don't let anyone know about this." And she promised.

The hospital was a teaching hospital, where a crew of students and a doctor would make their daily rounds and review each patient bedside. So I had all these 20 first-year medical students looking at me and discussing gonorrhea like I wasn't even there. It felt so humiliating. I had never heard of sexually transmitted diseases before, I was living in a different world—one that I was now noticing.

At this point in my life *acceptance* was my turning point. It was, sadly, my only defense to maintain my sanity. I was released in two days from the hospital with antibiotics and with one mission on my agenda—find Walter. We had been on and off since he'd come home from the war. And with his new friends, we were more off than on lately; it wasn't like it used to be before.

I got him alone a couple of days after I got out of the hospital and asked him if he'd ever cheated on me when he was on layover in New York before coming home to me. Then I asked him if he'd ever been treated for gonorrhea, because I was just hospitalized for it. I explained that it could last in a woman's womb for up to six months with no symptoms and pointed out that he was home about that time frame.

He said he was sorry. He'd thought just he had it and had gone to the doctor for antibiotics. He also elaborated, explaining that, after they'd landed in New York, he and all his war buddies had gone to a place in New York where there were plenty of hookers on the street begging for money in exchange for sex. Naturally, he said, all the guys—himself included—had jumped at the chance.

I knew at this time in my life that what had gotten me into this mess was that I had let myself fall in love with the wrong guy. I finally realized it. And here came my guilt problem once more. Why did he have to go to hookers when he was only one day away from home and seeing me? Why had he not told me he had the disease so I could have been checked out by a doctor and not gone through the humiliation of being hospitalized? Why?

That night and all the next week I thought long and hard for the first time in my life about me. I was twenty years old now. I could stay as I was and live a miserable life forever. Or I could change things around, get out of here, and start a new life. I knew I needed a break before I broke down.

The decision was made with no more guilt or remorse. My two sisters had moved out to Nevada, and I decided I had saved enough money to get a new apartment here. But I changed my mind and called them up, asking if I could join them. They welcomed me with open arms!

I felt bad quitting my job at the bank in Boston, but at least I'd finished school and had good references so I could get a good job in Nevada. I knew I was tainted, but that did not get in the way of my being conservative and clean-cut as they said back in the '70s. I was beginning to feel comfortable in my own skin for the first time in twenty years.

Inner silence / inner rage lay dormant. And when I got to Nevada, I got a good business job, bought a car, and eventually one of my sisters and I got an apartment together. I lived there for approximately two years and enjoyed every minute of it. Strangely, I never heard from Walter or any of the other girls.

When I arrived in Nevada, I felt like Dorothy in *The Wizard of Oz*. I was looking at the inner child inside of me and felt I was all four characters, with many lessons learned. I'd learned courage like the Cowardly Lion; I was not afraid anymore. And like the Tin Man, I still had my heart, which I was finally nurturing. As for the Scarecrow, I considered that, by going back to school, I had a good brain that enabled me to get a good job. Most of all, I began to love and trust, because like Dorothy, I had family. It was there all the time growing up in me. I wasn't going to shut up anymore.

Even though this was the hardest lesson I had to learn, I was able to make my own choices now and stick to them. I was free. And once I'd landed in Nevada, I found some inner peace! I'm not saying moving to a different location is the answer. I'm saying there comes a time in your life when you must say, "Enough."

The next two chapters are important for me to share. They depict how I actually survived through the traumas I endured at ages fifteen, sixteen, and seventeen. They explain how someone behind the scenes of my guilt was building up my self-esteem and courage so that I could survive and know that I was better than the cruelty I'd been dealt! I pay this tribute to my hero now because I finally found the answers to the question I'd always been asking. And that was, How did I ever survive without succumbing to mental illness or drugs?

I finally can see how I was given the self-esteem and courage to carry on to better things in life. Read on now. Maybe my story will enlighten you and help you to find your hero or to notice that, along your journey, you did have a hero, God bless.

CHAPTER 10

Introduction to Finding Your Hero

Have you ever wondered what your life would have been if you had gone a different path? Many young adults didn't have a choice. Usually, it was the parents who chose which college they would go to or what vocation they would apply for. Perhaps such a decision was what brought you to the profession you thought you wanted, yet today you find yourself thinking about the "what-if." If so, do you find the possibilities playing over and over in your mind?

There are many what-ifs that people ask themselves from time to time. You might think, *What if I'd married that young man I had a crush on when I was eighteen years old?* Yes, I'm talking about the guy your parents did not agree was the right one for you. There are, I'm sure, many of us who, one time or another, have thought back to the choices we could have made and wondered whether different decisions could have led us to a more fulfilling life. Otherwise, we wouldn't be thinking about that what-if.

You can even look back on some of the people you were buddies with and how they came and went, even from childhood to this very moment. Could they have made an impact on you that would have altered your future? There are many influences that played into making us who we are today.

For example, did you know that, from the womb till the age of two, you are predominantly in a delta brain wave state? This is known as the more primal brain activity that operates from an area of instinct. You are limited in conscious thought because you are operating on instinct at this stage. It's true; the fetus has to prepare itself for the environment that he or she is about to be born into. So he or she processes the emotions of his or her mother as part of this development. It's instinctual.

Then between two and six years of age, children are operating predominantly in theta brain wave state. We can say that children in this stage are in "sponge mode." In this stage of life, children observe their surroundings to learn how to respond and act.

As five-year-olds, we form opinions about things like money, health, self-confidence, and love, among other things that can influence us for the rest of our lives. This is the time when kids soak up and retain everything they observe, which means they just accept it. They then respond to everything in an automatic way because what they saw about how to engage with the world and how the world works was programmed into their subconscious. What I'm saying is that we had beliefs that were already formed between birth and the age of six—which could be good or bad beliefs. It all boils down to how those first six years went and where or what defined your self-esteem.

What I'm alluding to is what we choose (or think we choose) to take on in our journey of life is partly due to our own DNA that makes us so unique. However, many people don't ask themselves what their purpose here on earth is.

So, what is your passion? What makes you happy or sad? Do you stay stuck in a day-to-day mindless routine—a "Groundhog Day"—just because it's secure, safe, and comforting? Or because you believe that change is not an option for you?

Let's just say you and you alone have this bag you carry around with you, and it's full of your formative years, all the way up to your present life. Now pull everything out of your bag so you can see, possibly, lots of regrets or resentments, too much negativity, or too much sadness. Maybe your bag is filled with stuff you don't remember. Or maybe its contents are so familiar you don't care to look at them. Do you retreat, never to exam those memories or emotions that could give you a clue to who are you today? Who influenced you the most for better or for worse?

There are many people who were, for you, both a negative and/or a positive influence. But do you really recognize all the good stuff or all the bad stuff that's in your bag?

For me, I've carried my bag and, for years, only pulled out all the bad stuff that I was born into, because, in many ways, the bad stuff is easier to believe if you were an adolescent and the victim of abuse.

And that's why I finally realized I should write this story—to give hope and insight so that you can take a leap of faith. Seek somewhere deep in your memory bag to find your "Aha moment," which can give you a new light to quell the darkness you are possibly in. You can see that everything that's happened thus far has only been a detour. And you can know now that you owe it to yourself to find out who you were meant to be. That is my wish for you.

This story here is one of inspiration for those who depend only on themselves, which is a lonely place to be. Sharing my own story and experiences will help others and lead them to their true selves. There is a hero in your bag. It could be yourself who was the hero. Or when you truly look into your memory bag, you may find you had another hero too.

My wish is that you seek and acknowledge your memory bag as a significant tool. It can be a tool that enables you, when all is said and done, to say to yourself, *it's my time*. And there'll be no room for the what-if. You'll now have found your passion and purpose. And who knows? Maybe your bag is now empty so that you can create your own new one.

CHAPTER 11

Finding Your Hero

I am fast-forwarding just to help you understand my journey after the three rapes, after ten years of counseling, and after yet encountering more traumas, such as my divorce just to name one of many. I should have listened to my own advice then and gone for more counseling, as old and new triggers were present. But I didn't. It was about ten years later that I found myself in a mental hospital, not remembering what had triggered me to that point. I'd never entertained suicide before. But this one night, while my adult children were out, I had decided I could no longer deal with my demons anymore, so I swallowed a bunch of pills and thought I was going to heaven!

Luckily, my son came home unexpectedly and found me and dialed 9-1-1. This is another regret I will carry with me in my bag of inner silence / inner rage. I was forty-eight years old at the time and missed my old therapist Alice so much. I knew I had to reach out and again seek help.

Luckily for me, I sought help and was, once again, graced with a therapist the same age as me. Beth and I hit it off right away. And after I told her my story, she couldn't get over how I'd survived up to that point. She directed me, sustained me, and lovingly cared for me as an empathic ear, listening intensely to everything I spoke of. She actually encouraged me to continue my passion for writing and photography. So in a way, she was like Alice in many ways. Alice was one of my heroes and now I have been blessed with Beth, and to this day, I still see her once a week. There's never a dull moment in my life for sure.

As I drove home after our session, I reflected on what we'd discussed and how I'd missed the value of that talk we'd had. It came to me like an epiphany.

You see, I'd had a troubled life full of traumas. Remembering them and opening up to talking about them, I see (as do others) that it's a wonder how I've survived or, even better, continue surviving. How did I portray a woman of resilience for all my long years without a breakdown? How did I avoid being messed up in the head? Becoming a drug addict? An alcoholic? Getting addicted to anything that would numb the pain of my past? I even sometimes wonder myself why I didn't go insane—until I reflect back to Jane, my boss at the hospital where I worked.

I sat and talked to my current therapist, Beth, about a time in my life that was good, yet one I'd never talked about before. It was as if my therapist was saying the same exact words I'd heard before from my boss at my first job at the hospital. Why didn't I remember those lovely and kind words from two people who admired me first Jane then Anne? Did I habitually reject the good things about me? Did I not believe in them? Do I only remember the bad things in my life and focus on how to fix them? Where is the emotion I should be feeling? Why was I always living in a bubble?

During this particular session, my therapist Beth and I were talking about the first job I ever had. I was telling her that I'd quit high school just before I turned sixteen in September, 1965 because of the gang rape I'd endured at the hands of boys who all went to this new school I was to attend and how I couldn't imagine seeing my rapists every day. I was terrified of going to school and of them approaching me again. So I asked my mom if I could quit and go to work to help pay the bills. My dad was not home. He was, at the time, in jail for cashing bad checks. So my mom agreed.

I told her how my very first job was working in the kitchen of a hospital near our apartment, making it easy for me to walk to work. I mentioned that my mother also worked there at the hospital in the housekeeping department, washing floors, making beds, and so on. And I added that the best part of the job was that I could take home all the leftover food from the kitchen, which was a big deal to me, as there was hardly ever any food there at home.

This was where my story unfolded. You see, whenever I heard a certain song, "The Rose" by Bette Midler, I would sing that song word for word in my car at the top of my lungs (particularly the line, "Did you ever know that you're my hero?"). But I sang without any emotion tied to myself or any memory of anyone having been my hero. I always told myself I had no hero; that was certain. As in the song that Whitney Houston sings, "The Greatest Love of All" (which is basically telling the same message about heroes), "I never had a hero, no one to look up to, a lonely place to be so I learned to depend on me."

Well, there I was, telling my therapist about how I would be so proud to tell all the kitchen staff, even the managers, about my latest poem and how I would read it to them. I guess I was planting a seed that I had no clue I was growing right in my own back door. Even the secretary to the administrator of the hospital heard about the girl in the kitchen and read some of her beautiful poems.

One day, I was called down to the secretary's office. I was very apprehensive and thought I'd done something wrong and was going to be told off about writing my poems at work. I entered her office, humble and shaking.

She put her arms across her chest and said, "So, you're the kitchen girl with the lovely poems? Please have a seat."

We talked about my writing and why I didn't stay in school. (I just told her my dad was in jail for cashing bad checks, and I wanted to help my mom with the bills.) She told me that I was very gifted, elaborating on how much she admired my poems and writing. Then she offered me a better job, moving me from a dead-end job in the kitchen to being in charge of the mail room, as no one was managing the mail room at the time. The position came with a twenty-five-cent raise.

I was so excited. It was the first time someone was building up my confidence, adding a tiny speck of hope for my self-esteem. I especially appreciated this, as she must have known I had none. She gave me the confidence I'd needed for so long.

Of course I took the new position. And working in the mail room, I was happy. There was no more kitchen uniform and no more hairnet, which I hated wearing. Not to mention, I could do my own thing in terms of how to organize and deliver the mail. I was quite empowered.

The story here literally grows now. After just a couple of months in the mail room, I got the system up and running very efficiently, with smooth distributions to the other allocated offices throughout the hospital. And I'd managed to cut the hours previous employees had needed to complete the task in half.

Well, Jane, the administrator's secretary, had known I could do it, and she told me so. I was called to her office for the second time within three months now. She praised my work and capabilities and encouraged me to set my standards higher. She offered me the switchboard job, covering the day shift, as the woman who was the operator was moving far away. The position was opened to me even though I knew nothing about the job.

Naturally, I said yes. And of course, again, the promotion came with a terrific salary boost. Once more, Jane was building my self-esteem foundation without me even noticing it.

Everyone loved me as the switchboard operator. I became very professional, and my clothes were impeccable. I was copying Jane's attire; how I'd admired her conservative style. My happy me and my happy voice resonated when I had to speak on the loudspeaker's intercom to reach someone. For example, I would announce, "Mr. Sal Troyli, please report to the administrator's office." Or I would be looking for a doctor who was making her rounds to tell her she had a phone call and to dial 5.

Don't forget, my reader, cell phones were not invented yet. OMG! I was manually plugging cords into a wired board—aha, *switchboard*; the word was the appropriate description for the process of connecting and transferring all calls manually.

Jane watched me grow up so quickly and would always smile at me and stop to chat with me about what was new in my life. I always knew how concerned she was and that she genuinely cared for me.

And now, for the third time, there was another call for me to report to Jane's office in administration. I was very nervous this time; I do remember that meeting quite well. As I sat down in front of her desk, she proceeded to tell me again how smart and gifted I was, how fast I'd caught onto anything I'd needed to learn for all the different jobs and duties I'd accomplished in one year. She crossed her arms again across her chest and leaned into me from across the desk. Looking straight into my eyes, she said softly, "Kathy, I have a great offer and opportunity for you. It will enable you to make more money and to advance in your career as a professional employee." Then she became serious and added, "However, there is one request I will ask of you. And you must promise me you will honor my wish no matter what." She leaned back into her chair and waited a long moment. Then she leaned forward once again. "Okay, here's the deal."

There was a position coming up soon to work with the head nurse in the admitting department. Normally, this job would go to one of the hospital's nurse's aides, who were schooling to become nurses. But Jane had talked to her boss, the administrator—the top and highest person running this hospital—and she'd told Jane she could offer the position to me. If I was 100 percent sure I could handle the position, I could have it! I would be assisting the head nurse in the duties of admitting new patients and caring for them on their way to their hospital rooms and managing the important paperwork that went along with that process.

I sat there in shock. I was a high school dropout and knew nothing about nursing. But I kept silent as I stared into Jane's pretty brown eyes, searching for the why. And this was where and when I started to believe her and her confidence in me—that I could do anything if I believed in myself.

Jane then told me her wish and the condition that would benefit me and my future career, as she had tremendous faith that I could do anything once I put my mind to it. Once again she leaned forward with her arms across her chest. "Here's the deal," she said.

Jane had heard of a very new pilot program that would commence the September of that year. It was the first of its kind, and she said I was surely a candidate for it. This new program was called a "work-study program" and it would be administered by the public school system. It required a student who had quit school for whatever reason to come back to school at whatever grade level the student had previously been at upon quitting.

The students enrolled in the program would go to school for four hours every day five days a week. The school would then assign each student to a job in the Metropolitan area for the other half of the day. The school would monitor the students' job performance, along with their progress in school subjects and their grades. Plus, during the course of the year, the students would complete all the major courses they would have had if they hadn't quit school. After the required hours and courses were completed, students would graduate, just as they would have from their previous high school, receiving honor roll certificates if they earned it, plus all their credits, their high school diplomas, and a guaranteed job placement once they graduated.

Jane thought I would do well in courses involving business and accounting, and she would provide the recommendation I would need to enter this new program.

It didn't take me long at all to answer her and show her my enthusiasm and happiness, because I loved learning now, thanks to her. She smiled at me, with the love of a parent I thought. I've never seen anyone show me this type of all-out backing. And so we both agreed. It was not professional to give your boss a hug, even though I wanted to hug Jane, so we shook hands for a bit. And then she said with a big smile, "That's my girl."

The bittersweet part of this story is all about growth and letting go of something you find comforting. Once I started school that September, I no longer could work for Jane or the hospital. Part of the work-study program entailed us students working wherever the school assigned us. In my case, that September upon entering tenth grade, I was assigned to work at a bank in Boston in the foreign exchange department. Talk about a challenge!

Working with Mrs. Harrison, the head nurse in the admitting department at the hospital, that summer was fun. I learned so much about the patients, their sickness, and their family lives. I learned empathy at a very young age just from that one short time in my life over that summer.

When September came, I felt so sad, and I told Jane I didn't want to go. Jane, being Jane, said calmly, gently, and lovingly, "Remember you promised to honor my wishes?"

"Yes," I said, tears welling up into my eyes.

"Well," she said, "I'm asking this of you because you are a gifted, talented, and remarkable young lady, who one day will look back at this moment and whisper to herself, 'Yes, I did it. I did it, Jane.' You will thank me for believing in you and letting you go, knowing that I had the faith that you needed to see in your own self-worth. And everything you dreamed of will come to you; you will be a better person for this."

I visited Jane many times over the next two years of going to school and working in Boston. She even had me over to her house for lunch one time. Jane never married or had children, but I never asked her why.

At the end of school when graduation time came, I was wondering why I had not heard from Jane, as I'd invited her to my graduation. Then I received a call from Jane's brother Harold. He told me that Jane had passed away just the other day after a long bout of cancer, which she'd never told anyone about. He said that Jane had asked him to call me once she has gone and to tell me I was the one who'd kept her alive and happy for those past two years and that she knew I had a wonderful professional road ahead of me and to never look back. She asked that I continue to honor her wishes with one more wish, and that was for me to live abundantly! I was devastated and felt alone again.

After leaving the session with my therapist Beth that day while driving home, I did not realize what I was really unveiling. Until that day—as I reflected back on my conversation with Jane about that first job and how she had given me the opportunity to go on and make a better life for myself through job advancements—I had not seen it.

Now my thoughts took me by surprise. Bette Midler's song "The Rose" came on my car radio. At the words, "Did I ever tell you you're my hero," I had to pull off the road. I sat there crying softly, remembering Jane's beauty and the gift that she gave to me. I saw now, thirty years later, that I really did have a hero all along.

I looked up to the heavens and said out loud, "Jane, can you hear me? I wanted to tell you that *You are my hero*. I'm sorry I never opened up my heart or reflected on all the gifts you gave me in order to succeed in life. You healed me, Jane. I shall treasure this memory of you now and promise to read and reflect on it more often."

I was working at the hospital—at ages fifteen, sixteen, and seventeen—during a very difficult period. Those were the years of my three rapes, which were buried in the world of my inner silence / inner rage. But it was also a time I kept myself busy at the hospital. All along, in the background, Jane, my hero, was working on building my self-worth and my low self-esteem—encouraging me that I could do anything I wanted if I just focused on it.

Jane never knew about my three rapes. I kept those bad memories in my bag of inner silence / inner rage. I truly think now she must have known something bad had happened in my past. And that was how I truly survived!

I guess I'm hoping I can be the hero for someone out there too; it's a precious gift, indeed.

EPILOGUE

Traumas can be defined as shock, an ordeal, confusion, violence, emotional disturbance, terror, horror, and an outburst. To me, there is only one way I can describe trauma—it's an experience that moves your whole being into feeling numb and shocked and shutting down. The death of a baby, for example, is a tragedy you would experience as a trauma. Ask a soldier, fireman, nurse, doctor, or policeman what he or she thinks defines trauma. It all boils down to the *experience* and how it shocks you and haunts you every time a trigger reminds you of that experience. For some people who've experienced trauma, until they can get help and acknowledge the experience, they just black out.

Perhaps you've experienced an event that was so horrific you almost threw up. Your heart was beating fast, sweat poured from your brow, and you couldn't catch your breath. You couldn't run. You were frozen in the experience. This was what happened to me when I was gang-raped. I could not remember anything once I blacked out. I only recall running, crying, raging! This is what a very dark trauma can lead you into.

Some of us who've gone through traumas try to forget that pain. We black it out or bury it way down inside so we don't recollect the experience at all. This is why I'm sharing my story. I want to help people be more aware of the signs that trauma brings to their lives—sooner rather than later. I want to help them avoid what I experienced in my early adolescence—how we try to think something is "no big deal," but it is a big deal and leads to permanent damage if not addressed.

That was where I'd been for many years—out of control and enduring the damage of not having dealt with the traumas of my past. But when you don't face your trauma, just as in a nightmare, the "once upon a time"— your past—comes at you full throttle eventually. I was utterly frustrated, and I needed some answers. That's when I sought out professional help. I was lucky to get two therapists who clicked with me right away. But please don't feel stuck with just one. If you don't feel comfortable with the first therapist you work with, it is your God-given right to keep seeking the right therapist or groups that will lead you on your way to discovering who you really are and why.

It's a merry-go-round, believe me, and I needed to see and stop the damage of my trauma with or without help. My marriage was good for the first five years. Then the obsessing, the drinking, the not working, and the abusiveness started. Attending Al-Anon group sessions—whatever the subject of discussion—was my first step in saying, "Enough."

Hopefully you get to do this or at least read some books on the subject of whatever trauma or difficult situations you're going through. You'll be surprised, as I was once I started asking questions—how much help you'll get.

Talk to someone about your trauma. Read books on the subject of your choice; there are many out there. Get some counseling, enroll in a self-help class, and join an organization that deals specifically with whatever your trauma is.

If I had to guess, my reader, you've had more than just one trauma. Does it ever go away? No, but what does happen over time is that you become more tuned into it and more aware. You're knowing how to handle the triggered trauma increases, and you start to heal. At least that was what happened for me.

I have learned through years of therapy (I had a lot of issues) that I finally could trust. I joined a self-help class, a self-assertiveness class, and a self-esteem class, along with Al-Anon classes. You name it. I was on a marathon, and it was exhilarating.

But I only partially healed. After I divorced, I blamed myself, not knowing that it was my alcoholic husband and his abusiveness that were untenable. I didn't connect the dots between his behavior and that of my own father. I just didn't see that I had married a man just like my father, and that was not good. I was in denial and steeped in too much depression.

I blamed myself for splitting up my so-called happy home and family. I was just re-traumatizing myself, pushing all the bad things going on deep down into the very core of myself. You see, I had mastered my "inner silence." Little did I know that this divorce was the trigger that made some of my secrets resurface?

Being a single parent hurt me the most, but I would try to keep my three boys together. We were never going to leave and move out of the very foundation I had built—the foundation of stability I'd constructed in my mind and the brick-and-mortar foundation of my house. I was not going to be like my parents and move eight times in my kids' seventeen years at home. I dug in my heels on this one and got three jobs to pay the large mortgage and everything else that went with it. I could never depend on my ex-husband to give me any money, as I knew he would never find a real job. Little did I realize that I'd become a workaholic, and my kids didn't know me anymore. I had become the sole breadwinner, with all the setbacks that came along with that role.

The real inner silence / inner rage began when I was very young. I can recall it a thousand times, and it's always been the same. *From Inner Silence / Inner Rage to Inner Peace* is about my journey, my life, my experiences, and me. I have changed the names, houses, towns, and facilities. Everyone has his or her own story; this is mine.

My journey and traumas wrap around four decades of my life up to now. I am at peace with myself and all that has happened now because I opened up my emotions to the right books, therapists, classes, and organizations.

I do give myself credit for seeking the right help I needed, but I am eternally grateful to the people who cared and guided me in the right direction of self-healing. In addition, the many books I've read have helped me enormously to stay focused and on the right path, which gave me the courage to heal.

As noted earlier, I truly believe that I would have been a manic-depressive or a severe drug or alcohol addict—a nonfunctional person—had it not been for my precious collection of self-help, soul-searching, and spiritual and uplifting books. Another reason for writing this story is to help anyone out there who needs a little nudge (and then a few more nudges) to see that it's not him or her. I hope to show such a person that it's possible to move from self-deprivation to self-love and that there are books out there that can prove it. Go to the library; it's free! You can find courage, solace, and help through stories of healing your inner child without taking a pill.

My journey might be just the beginning for you to recognize your own. And I love you dearly, my reader, for your courage to understand that there is something wrong and to read a book that can help you see yourself through the darkness in your mind.

I hope and pray that my quest to write my story will help others out there who've had one or many traumas gain confidence and strength to carry their torches of freedom to the very end. Then you can be on another journey. You can help yourself heal, forgive yourself, and help others on their way too.

No matter what you think trauma might be, I hope I have at least let you recognize your experience as your own trauma. I hope I've shown with this work I'm now sharing with you that you can unpack your inner silence / inner rage and find your inner peace.

Today, I am a woman who has shattered her own silence. I am a victim no longer. I am a victorious survivor, and you can be also.

I hope I reach you, my reader. I hope I can be a part of guiding and helping you through your own journey. God bless you.

I have mentioned a number of steps toward finding inner peace in each and every chapter, and I've compiled them here. (Remember, though, I am not a doctor, just your mentor.) Here are the steps you might take and the references you may want to ponder:

1. Be totally aware of your gut feelings and intuition. When you feel uncomfortable, get out of whatever situation you're in as fast as you can. (For instance, if I'd had enough self-esteem and thought better of myself when I was a teen, I never would have gotten into those three cars. I never would have been raped three times. I would have said no and moved away very quickly from the situation.) Get to a public place, where there are phones or people to help you.

2. Always confide in someone if you've experienced a trauma. Talk to a loved one or a close friend. Having someone you can trust by your side is important. Then new doors will begin to open. Action is the key.

3. Don't carry on the shame of your caretakers. Remember to make this your mantra: "I am not responsible for others' actions." Teach your children, yourself, and your mate healthy habits of physical, emotional, and mental behavior. Base those habits on respect and, most of all, love.

4. You will always be responsible for your own accountability, so live your life with integrity. Start trusting your own actions.

5. Surround yourself with good people. Positive and upbeat people wear off on us in a most positive way. Maybe find a role model or mentor.

6. Stay away from friends and others with addictions. You cannot cure them. Only when you feel worthy and knowledgeable about addictions can you offer them aid. Then you can help them by providing references. Otherwise, they can pull all the energy out of you.

7. Keep searching for the hidden passion that is longing to be free. It's in there. Ask yourself every day what excites you and really feel that. Always when you wake up in the morning show appreciation and gratitude for the things you already have, and more good things will start to show up. Be grateful you are ready to embrace your new day. And if you don't know what that is, then it's time to find out who you really are and where you want to go on this God-given journey.

Lightning Source UK Ltd.
Milton Keynes UK
UKHW011105111120
373211UK00008B/559/J